Celeste Charland is a shamanic teacher, practitioner, professional coach and facilitator, and painter—now residing in Ottawa, Ontario, Canada. Over the past 20 years, Celeste has walked the path of the shaman and of direct revelation. Her teachers include Sandra Ingerman, Betsy Bergstrom, and the Foundation for Shamanic Studies. Celeste has an active shamanic practice offering guidance and workshops in Canada, the United States, and distance healing worldwide. She is also a follower of the teachings of Swami Satchidananda and an active student of the Integral Approach. She is also an ordained Inter-spiritual Minister with One Spirit Inter-Spiritual Alliance located in New York.

This book is dedicated to my parents,
Edouard and Jeanne Charland. I miss them both dearly.

To my husband, Gilles, and to my sons, Justin, Chad, Sean,
and Alexandre. This is a love song for you.

Celeste Charland

SHAMANIC VOYAGES OF SELF-DISCOVERY

A Book of Journeys

AUSTIN MACAULEY PUBLISHERS™

LONDON · CAMBRIDGE · NEW YORK · SHARJAH

Ordering Information:
Quantity sales: special discounts are available on quantity purchases by corporations, associations, and others. For details, contact the publisher at the address below.

Publisher's Cataloging-in-Publication data
Charland, Celeste
Shamanic Voyages of Self-Discovery: A Book of Journeys

ISBN 9781643788272 (Paperback)
ISBN 9781643788265 (Hardback)
ISBN 9781645365303 (ePub e-book)

Library of Congress Control Number: 2019918360

www.austinmacauley.com/us

First Published (2020)
Austin Macauley Publishers LLC
40 Wall Street, 28th Floor
New York, NY 10005
USA

mail-usa@austinmacauley.com
+1 (646) 5125767

This book could not have been written without the help and guidance of many people. First and foremost, I thank all of my teachers, both in ordinary reality and non-ordinary reality. I cherish their ongoing love, support, and guidance. Special thanks to my very first shamanic teachers, Kelly and Sharon Van Raalte. A big heart-felt thank you to my clients, who support me in this work and remind me how to show up every day. Thanks to my husband, Gilles, for his ongoing patience, understanding, and unconditional love. Thank you to my four amazing sons, Justin, Chad, Sean, and Alexandre. I am so blessed that you have chosen me as your mother. Thanks to my daughters-in-law, France and Selin. You are inspiring models for women. And finally, thanks to my two grandchildren, William and Amélie. You make my heart sing and teach me every day how to feel joyful and grateful.

Reviews

"Once you discover what a shamanic practitioner *does,* the word 'enough' instantly loses its meaning. You always want more: *more* healing, *more* classes*, more* powerful teachings, *more* journeys, *more* glimpses into the very Weave of the Universe...

When an experienced shamanic practitioner writes a book, you want her to share her best-kept secrets: her life-time collection of the most healing, most life-changing journeys.

Celeste Charland has done just that. By means of this book, she delivers the Cosmos to your door on a dinner plate! Devour this book! Embrace the journeys! And remember that the carbon footprint for soul travel is zero!"

— Imelda Almqvist, international teacher of Sacred Art and Northern Tradition Shamanism, author of *Natural Born Shamans: A Spiritual Toolkit for Life* and *Sacred Art: Where Art Meets Shamanism*

"In this wonderful gem, *Shamanic Voyages of Self-Discovery: A Book of Journeys*, Celeste Charland provides great insight into the heartfelt intentions of Shamanic Journeying and its ability to be transformative. Ms. Charland is talented in conveying how profound and powerful healing journeys can be."

— Marilyn Graman
psychotherapist, shaman practitioner, author

Table of Contents

Foreword

I met Celeste Charland when she was a student in my two-year program *Teacher Training in Shamanic Journeying, Healing and Medicine for the Earth*. In order to qualify for this intensive program, students have to demonstrate that they have a strong connection with spirit animals and guides. Celeste had walked the path of the shaman with humility, intent, and integrity for many years before I met her and she clearly has a gift to do this work, or more precisely 'spirit' has chosen her to do this work. For Celeste, shamanism is not a practice, it is a way of life that she embraces every breathing moment. That is why I am proud and honored to list Celeste on my international shamanic teachers' website. Celeste Charland is no longer a student of mine, but is a peer and trusted colleague.

Shamanism is the first universal spiritual practice known to humankind. The practice dates back tens of thousands of years and was practiced all over the world. The word 'shaman' comes from the Tungus tribe in Siberia and holds meanings such as 'spiritual healer' or 'one who knows,' or 'one who sees in the dark.' A shaman is a man or woman who uses the ability to see 'with the strong eye' or 'with the heart' to travel into hidden realms. The shaman interacts directly with helping spirits to address the spiritual aspect of illness and perform healing ceremonies such as soul retrievals, retrieve lost power, perform depossessions, as well as remove spiritual blockages. Shamanism teaches us that everything that exists is alive and has a spirit. Shamans speak of a web of life that connects all of life and the spirit that lives in all things. It is a system of direct revelation. All shamans might describe experiences differently and how the different experiences are interpreted and seen by others, which is the reason they are so beautiful.

In Shamanic Voyages of Self Discovery, Celeste gives us a glimpse of her very real and unique experience as a modern shamanic practitioner. She shows us how shamanism is the essence of alternative medicine, helping clients in finding ways to restore balance and harmony in their life and creating a positive present and future.

In our increasingly complex and ever-changing world, it becomes more and more difficult to find one own's sense of balance and harmony. This book is so needed right now as more and more people search for a sense of meaning. We are all hungry to connect with more than what we experience with our ordinary senses in the material world. This compilation of journeys is a reminder that reconnecting with love and compassion is our sole (soul) purpose. This book will inspire you to awaken or re-awaken to the potential of your self-healing. I am delighted to include this book in my collection of shamanic pearls.

Sandra Ingerman, MA
Shamanic teacher and author of 12 award-winning books on shamanism, including:

Soul Retrieval: Mending the Fragmented Self and
The Book of Ceremony: Shamanic Wisdom for Invoking the Sacred into Everyday Life.

Preface

We live in interesting times. The beliefs, structures, and frameworks that seemed to support us for so long are becoming fragmented all around the world. Over the past few years, clients who reached out to me use words like: a search for meaning, a sense of longing, feeling numb, feeling disconnected, feeling beside themselves etc. I believe that as our world shifts and becomes more and more complex and fast-paced, there is a deep yearning to go within, to find balance. There are so many choices, so many confusing messages. I notice a need from young and old to reconnect with the self. There is a strong urge to re-discover one's inner compass and sense of direction. The shamanic path is a path of direct revelation. On this path, each and every human being is invited to connect with his or her own inner wisdom, to remember who they were before they were born and who they will be after they have passed. By connecting to one's true authentic self, we open ourselves up to cosmic wisdom, the knowing field, the ancestors' circle, Oneness—whatever we choose to call it—and we re-discover our purpose. In a world where religions have become more about the politics of men than the connection with the Divine, in a world where it is difficult to trust what we see, hear, and sense, integrating the ancestral teachings of shamanism brings us right back to where we started—ourselves.

The journeys provided in this book are just a few examples of how, as a shamanic practitioner, I am helping others re-connect with their own power so that they may show up fully in their world. I do this quietly, every day, one person at a time so that they may, in turn, do it for others.

About This Book

This book humbly offers teachings and wisdom chosen from hundreds of shamanic journeys I have done for myself and on behalf of clients over the past 20 years. Using the ancestral traditional method of shamanic journeying, I reach an altered state of consciousness to connect with spirit animals, guides, and teachers, and to access wisdom for myself and my clients. Although I have received permission to share these journeys, names have been changed to protect the identity of my clients.

Journeys are presented in four categories:

- **Self-Healing Journeys**: these are journeys I have done for myself over the past 20 years;
- **Healing Journeys for Clients**: these are journeys I have done on behalf of clients over the past 20 years. They include the initial contact made by the client, the diagnostic journey I did on their behalf, the healing journey or journeys, and a brief check-in providing information received from the client after the journey;
- **Dismemberment Journeys**: these are journeys I have done, where a classic spontaneous

dismemberment took place, or a dismemberment was the express intent of the journey;

- **Death and Dying Journeys**: these are journeys on behalf of clients or myself, involving a dying or deceased loved one.

Although each journey provides wisdom for myself and/or for each client, it has been my experience that healing stories are universal. Many times, during one of our shamanic gatherings, someone shares a journey and others in the circle feel it is also meant for them, and it triggers some significant healing. By sharing these journeys, I am hoping that they will have the same effect on the reader. The journeys may move around your own healing energy and/or may remind you of your own journey home.

***

Introduction:
A Brief Personal History

Awakening

I have always been a bit of an odd duck. I was a very quiet child, preferring books to the company of others. I was keenly aware of the world around me, and from a very young age, always felt like everything around me was alive. I talked to trees and plants, and even gave names and human attributes to things. I thought everyone saw the world this way, until I was told I had a very vivid imagination. I read voraciously, and at around the age of 11, the librarian at our local public library, who knew me very well by then, gave me an adult's library card because she said I had outgrown the children's section. I was delighted to discover so many new books. My favorite section was philosophy, psychology, and spirituality. Being from a family of nine children, no one bothered to check what I was reading.

An incident occurred to me at around the age of twelve that was to be a sign of things to come later in life. I was walking home from school by myself one day when I heard someone calling my name. I turned around but there was nobody there. I stopped and waited. I started walking again and the voice started talking to me again. It said, *'Get on with the business of learning as much as you can, so that you can focus on your life's purpose. You are no longer an innocent child now, remember who you are.'* I had no idea what that meant, and feeling a bit frightened, I ran home. As it happened, my father was home that afternoon and he noticed that I looked a bit pale. He asked me what was wrong. I shared my experience with him. He listened in silence, then he told me not to share this with anyone else, and that if it happened again, I could share it with him. For some reason I thought I had done something wrong. I lost my innocence that day. I started to look at the world differently and felt a sense of urgency to grow up. Life became busy and I forgot all about the voice.

Self-Healing and Self-Discovery

Life has been good to me. I was always an A-grade student and excelled at whatever I set my mind to. Like many women of my generation, I married the first man that paid attention to me. We had two amazing sons but, as I began the work of finding my voice and discovering who I needed to be, I knew I could not stay in this marriage. Once I knew I could be financially self-sufficient, I walked out on my husband with my suitcase of clothes and the only two beings that truly mattered to me, my 6-year-old and 4-year-old sons. My career as a Human Resources Executive began to take off, and for the first time in my life, I started to go inward to discover who I really was. I did a lot of self-healing during this period: I worked through my disease to please, I deconstructed and rebuilt my belief system, and I learned to love myself. And, finally, at the age of 30 I started to reconnect with that little girl who had heard a voice so long ago, inviting her to make a difference. After I finished my Master's Degree in Education, I began to immerse myself in everything I could get my hands on that related to self-healing and personal development. I was fascinated with human beings and how they relate to each other. My HR work provided plenty of opportunities to study the human condition. I met a wonderful man who later became my husband and we became a blended family of 5, and two years later a family of 6.

Everything was great, until it wasn't. On the verge of turning forty years old, I suddenly started having recurring nightmares. I felt very alone, even in large group settings and with family. I felt numb and disconnected. Nobody, other than my husband, could guess that I was so distraught. During the day, it was easy. I just forgot about myself and worked on behalf of others. While I focused on my boys and my work, I did not have to focus on what was going on inside of me. But, at night, a deep feeling of despair would take hold of me. My husband tried to help by suggesting counselling or therapy work, but I had this deep sense of knowing that this was not a psychological issue. In spite of my attempts at meditation, yoga, prayer, sacred dancing, you name it… I still felt a deep sense of longing. I was never suicidal because there was always this small light inside of me that I knew was my life force. I could feel it even in my darkest hours. I just sensed that this light was trying to tell me something but I could not hear it clearly or make sense of it. I eventually shared my pain with my brother who recommended that I get in touch with a friend and a colleague that dealt with this sort of thing. I took her name and phone number and tucked the piece of paper in my purse. I convinced myself that, perhaps, I was working too hard and some well-deserved rest would make me feel better. The Holiday Season was soon approaching. Well, the Holiday Season came and went, and I remember feeling zero emotion about the whole thing. I knew I loved my husband, my boys, and my family, but I could not feel anything. I was scared.

One morning, as I was reaching in my purse for something, a piece of paper fell out. I picked it up and noticed the woman's name and number my brother had given me. Not wanting to give myself any excuse to back out, I immediately picked up the phone and called her. She invited me for tea that weekend. I started spending many afternoons with Kelly, who sat there and just listened. Then, one day, she told me about a workshop her sister was giving at the Edge in Algonquin Park in Northern Ontario. She said it was about shamanism. I told her I did not like that kind of woo-woo stuff, and I did not like talking about myself in that kind of setting. I did not know much about shamanism but I did not want to be one of "those bell-ringing granola people". She laughed and told me to check it out. I decided to sign up and paid the entire amount upfront so that I would not back out of it. I had never done anything like this before. When the weekend finally arrived, I drove the entire one-hour drive in silence debating whether I should just turn around. When I arrived at the retreat center, I was greeted by a wonderful compassionate woman. She was pure kindness and understanding. I was surprised to see about thirty-five people there, none with bells, or flowing dresses, or anyone remotely looking granola (whatever that meant).

I listened quietly while Sharon, our teacher for the weekend, explained a bit about shamanism. Then she invited us to experience our first shamanic journey. To the beat of her drum, we followed her instructions on how to reach an altered state of consciousness. From that very first drum beat, I was gone. I met a guide who showed me all kinds of wonderful things and, more importantly, for the first time in a very long time, I connected with this world. I felt like I had come home. We journeyed a lot that weekend and my world shifted. On my drive back home, I had to stop by the side of the road because I was crying so hard. I felt so relieved, so joyful. When I journeyed, I did not have any yearning or longing, all I felt was love and a deep sense of connection. When I got home that afternoon, I asked my husband if I looked the same. He laughed and said *'yes.'* I checked into the mirror. My face was the same, but I felt so different. I was no longer the same person. I wanted more.

I embarked on a journey, both physically and figuratively. I read everything I could about the ancestral teachings of shamanism. I signed up for every shamanic workshop I could get my hands on. This was early 2000s, so there was not much offered in Canada. Once I had taken everything on the East Coast of Canada, I signed up for workshops and programs in the U.S. More often than not I was one of a handful of Canadians. I enrolled in Michael Harner's Foundation for Shamanic Studies' two-week shamanic counseling in San Francisco, then the three-year program in Advanced Initiation in Shamanism and Shamanic Healing. I then wanted to learn with Betsy Bergstrom and signed up for her two-year Wheel of Life program at Pendle Hill, where I learned about ancestral teachings from the Egyptians, the Norse, and the Sami. I also honed my craft in compassionate de-possession, curse unravelling, and middle world journeys.

I then wanted to learn from one of the best shamanic teachers. I joined a group of like-hearted and like-minded people in Santa Fe to spend two years learning how to be a shamanic teacher with Sandra Ingerman. During all of those years of training, I learned so much from my human teachers, but as I journeyed and became familiar with the spirit world, I received a tremendous amount of wisdom and guidance from spiritual guides and teachers. I developed strong partnerships with these teachers. I slowly started connecting the dots and making sense of some of the many intuitive episodes and prophetic dreams I had experienced as a child. As I learned more and more about the way of the shaman, it became a way of being for me. I re-connected with myself and discovered that I have a gift.

From Self to Others

In the early years, my focus was on my own inward journey. But then, as I shared some of my experiences with friends and colleagues, they asked me to journey on their behalf. I was very reluctant at first. Although I had done more than 10 years of training with some of the best, and although I journeyed regularly for myself, I resisted doing it for others. This was to be the beginning of a constant battle with ego. I was in essence leading two lives, the life of a professional woman who was advising and coaching executives and management teams on reaching goals, organizational development and accountability, and the life of a shamanic being who was opening herself up to her intuition and to the guidance of ancestors, guides, and spirit animals. The more I embraced my inner changing landscape, the more my professional practice began to shift. As a senior executive once pointed out to me, after I had facilitated a particular difficult group session, *'I watch how you facilitate and how you bring the group along. What you do is beyond a skill set, what you do is art; I have never seen anyone do it this way.'* I shrugged off the compliment at the time, but as I thought about it days later, I realized that I was no longer separating my professional life from my personal being. I was showing up differently in the world. I journeyed to my guides to ask them how I should proceed. The message was clear, *"Get out of your own way, become the hollow bone; this is not about you, this is about your gift of being a portal for others."*

From that moment, I began saying yes. I started a shamanic practice and journeyed on behalf of clients: at first locally, then across Canada, then worldwide. Every time I do a diagnostic journey on behalf of a client, followed by healing journeys, I am in awe of the power and magic of this work. I do not know how any of it works really, but I trust it implicitly. And, I have found that my background in group dynamics and change management has helped me provide practical support to clients in integrating this healing in their every-day life.

In 2013, I entered seminary at the One Spirit Learning Alliance in New York. I was ordained as an Interfaith-Interspiritual Minister in 2015. The teachings I received in this amazing program gave me the confidence and additional tools to fully show up in this world to make a difference. At this time, I also fell in love with Ken Wilber's Integral Theory, which has become an integral part of my practice and of my path of growing up and waking up.

From Self to the Collective

As my shamanic practice thrived, I was getting requests to teach people on how to journey for themselves and to learn more about the way of the shaman. I soon realized that I had a gift to share. I started offering regular workshops and teachings. In spite of the success of these workshops, I wanted to create a space that was different than the current workshop framework the participants are used to. I wanted to create spaces where like-hearted people would feel empowered, where each individual's unique path would be honored, focusing less on content and more on the flow of things. I created the first "Non-community Community" gatherings in 2014. This monthly drop-in focuses on creating a safe and sacred container to allow participants to:

- go inward: to deepen personal inner work and spiritual development;
- go upward: to create meaning that is larger than ourselves, remembering our essence and higher self;
- go downward: to ground us in our "humanness," allowing us to connect to Mother Earth and to our human path, helping us navigate this reality;
- go across: that is, to contribute in a meaningful way to our communities, either individually or collectively.

These days, as our world is seemingly in a state of chaos, I am noticing that most of my clients have a deep longing for a sense of meaning and purpose, reconnecting with ancestral teachings.

As I embrace my eldership, I am more and more struck by the beauty of the ongoing dance between the self, the other, and the universe. My shamanic teachings and my humble understanding of integral theory have led me to this: it is all about honoring my relationship with self, my relationship with others, and my relationship with the universe, each and every moment. There is no destination, only an ever-unfolding journey.

***

Walking the Path of the Shaman: 5 Guiding Principles

This work is important to me. It has completely changed my life. Walking the path of the shaman is a constant way of being with myself, others, and Mother Earth. When my guides encouraged (pushed) me to get out of my own way and to start doing the work I was meant to do, it was important for me to trust my inner compass. In order to keep myself in a state of grace, humility, and integrity, I use five principles to guide my practice:

Principle 1: Be a Hollow Bone

Practitioners often use this expression from indigenous cultures. As a healing portal or conduit for others, in order to allow the healing energy to flow through, I have to constantly work on my own healing. Am I able to stand in my power (the bone) while allowing healing energy to flow clearly (the hollow)? If I am not aware of my own wounds, beliefs, biases, if I have not owned and embraced my own shadow pieces, how can I be a true guide for others? I work diligently and intentionally at being a clear vessel for myself and others by clearing my mind of expectation and reminding myself that, as a human being, I will be tempted to judge, to use ego, to filter, and to preach as an excuse to help others. It is not about my clients becoming more like me, it is about them becoming more like them. By being a hollow bone, I am reminded that everyone's journey is unique. The way of the shaman is a path of direct revelation, I am merely a conduit for a client to discover his or her own unique path.

Principle 2: Integrity and Impeccability, Always

Integrity and impeccability are extremely important to me. I do not journey on behalf of anyone else, including my husband, my children, and other loved ones, unless I get their express permission to do so. I always have a preliminary meeting (phone, Skype, or in person) with a client to explain what I do and what I do not do. I always get written permission to do a diagnostic journey, and further permission to do every healing journey. When I get this permission, I recognize the pact I am making to go and see their energy field and to get the help of compassionate spirits to move that energy around. Healing journeys are not always positive and joyful, they sometimes open up deep wounds. Journeying on behalf of a client could take one session, three months, one year or more. Clients need to be partners every step of the way. I am sometimes asked to do a journey on behalf of someone's husband, sick parent, or troubled teenage daughter. I do not do it without the express permission of the person I am asked to journey for.

From a shamanic perspective, healing does not necessarily mean a physical healing. Many of my clients have a family doctor (body), a psychotherapist (mind), and a shamanic practitioner (spirit) helping them. My goal is to help the client re-connect with his or her "spirit" or "essence". When I am asked to journey on behalf of a young child, a baby, or an Alzheimer's patient, I journey to my guides first to see if this is appropriate. When my mother was diagnosed with Alzheimer's, I journeyed to my guides and asked them if I could journey on her behalf. They gave me a flat no. I would return to them every year to see if the answer had changed. They always refused, until approximately six months before my mother passed, they gave me permission to journey to her. That journey is included in this book.

Impeccability also means that I do not share any of the journeys with anyone else. A client may share his or her journey as he or she pleases but it is not my place to do so. That is why this book could not have been written without first getting permission from my clients.

Principle 3: Trust the Wisdom Received

When I first started to do this work, I would sometimes get journeys that made absolutely no sense to me. At times, a client would show up and what had been planned as a one-hour session was finished in ten minutes. This made me uncomfortable. I worried about what the client would think: surely a healing session must mean a lot of pomp and ceremony, surely this issue that is so significant must need hours and hours to unravel. Well, it just does not work that way. I have found over and over again that the information I receive is exactly what is needed at that time. I have learned to convey the information in the journey **exactly** how I have received it, without interpreting, judging, or questioning. To this day, and every time I journey, after having done hundreds of journeys, I am in awe of this work. What makes no sense to me, makes sense to a client. When my guides tell me not to journey on a particular day or at a scheduled time, the pieces of the puzzle eventually fall into place. I have learned to trust my body and my intuition. I find that I sometimes start getting information on behalf of a client way before I have journeyed, sometimes in my dreams. By trusting the wisdom of my guides, for myself and others, I am able to honor the work, myself, and my client.

Principle 4: Get Out of the Way

Before I began doing this work on behalf of others, I felt great resistance. Part of that resistance stemmed from my own struggle with ego. The ego is tricky at times, because when I believe I have won the battle, I find that not wanting to do the work is just another form of ego. I have learned that this work is a true partnership with Spiritual Guides, and Teachers, and the client. When I doubt myself, or when I am asked to do something my mind struggles with: be it a workshop, a gathering, or a journey, I have found that journeying to my guides for wisdom is a great way to get out of my own way. After years of management and facilitating groups, I tend to analyze everything and to go to my head space first. By journeying on an issue or dilemma,

I find I can go to my heart space first which will then inform my head space. This allows me to get out of my own way.

Principle 5: Empower

Although many clients want me to tell them what a journey means and to get advice on what they should do, this is not my work. My work is to help clients re-connect with their own power. This is difficult for clients at times who just want answers. My professional training as a coach and facilitator helps me ask a client the tough questions to help them discover their own truth. I will often say to a client, *'This is your path, your journey; let me walk beside you for a while, let me tap into universal wisdom, the knowing field to help you see your own luminescence.'* Anything else would be disempowering.

Self-Healing Journeys

These journeys are self-healing journeys because they are journeys I did for myself, either with a specific intent, question, or problem in mind or just to feel more joy, to connect with my essence, or to feed my soul. As one goes to the gym or eats a healthy meal to nourish the body, or reads a book or attends a workshop to nourish the mind, I journey to feed my soul and to stay in balance.

Self-Healing Journey: Letting Go

I want to be able to journey to guides and teachers. I want to stop the monkey brain and the constant chatter and to re-connect with my essence. Please help me let go.

Celeste (1999)

Healing Journey for Celeste

Our canoe glides silently along the dark jungle river. The only sound is the swoosh of my guide's long wooden paddle pushing us forward. The darkness is engulfing everything. I sense the thick humid foliage on either shore. I imagine a night sky, but there are no stars, there is no moon. We float in silence. Our canoe makes a slight bump and my body lurches forward. My guide reaches for my hand and helps me out of the canoe. He turns and leaves. I am now alone on the shores of the river. I notice an old woman sitting in silence beside a campfire. I approach her and sit next to her. By the light of the fire, I can barely discern her features, but I know she is old... no, not old... ancient. Her body is fragile, yet I am afraid of her. She mumbles something and slowly gets up. She motions for me to follow her. We walk to the edge of the river. She bends down and starts to wash her hands. She motions for me to do the same. I bend over and start to wash my hands. Suddenly, and without warning, she shape-shifts into a crocodile and snatches my waist between her powerful jaws. I struggle but cannot get free. She brings me into the depths of the river and we plunge into the murky water. We roll and roll together, until I can no longer breathe, and I have totally lost all sense of direction. When my body becomes limp and I no longer know who or where I am, she whispers in my ear:

'Are you ready to listen now?'

Check-in with Celeste

This was one of my very first journeys back in 1999. At the time, I had been taught the technique of journeying and was eager to go. I found it difficult at times to get out of my own head. After this journey, all of me—my body, my mind, my senses, knew what it felt like to let go. Crocodile woman became a powerful, compassionate, and ruthless teacher for me.

Self-Healing Journey: Creative Abundance and Joy

I find I am stuck creatively. As an artist I have always been able to create. Sure, I sometimes go through dry spells but never for this long. I am afraid I may not be able to paint or write again. What if I have lost it? I am very sad and feel I have lost my way.

Celeste (2005)

Healing Journey for Celeste

I set out to meet Urd, Verdandi and Skuld to ask for creative abundance and joy. I circle the Tree of Life three times, then sit down and lean against its powerful trunk. As the sun rises, the three Norns show up and motion me to follow them. Before we leave, Verdandi puts up her closed fist and invites me to open it. I pry her fingers open and find three things: a seed, a small apple, and a dried prune. She laughs, then puts a finger to her lips indicating we have to walk in silence. After a while we reach a pond. The three of them ease themselves into the healing waters and cleanse themselves. They invite me to join them, but I am only allowed to wash my hands. After some time, Urd asks me what I want.

'Could you weave more creative abundance and joy into my life's tapestry?' I enquire.

'Which is it, creative abundance or joy?' asks Skuld.

'Both,' I reply.

'She asks for two threads,' chuckles Verdandi, *'how bold.'*

They soak in the pond in silence and I wait. Finally, Verdandi emerges and tells me to follow her. She gives me her basket to carry. She takes some star, sun, and moon dust, and says, *'This is for creativity.'* She then takes a bit of essence of buttercup, daisy and marigold and says, *'This is for joy.'* I then follow her to her spinning wheel and she spins them into two threads. She gives the threads to me. I thank her and ask her if I could wash her feet. She smiles and nods. As I finish wiping her feet, I suddenly find myself in Skuld's weaving room. She asks me to give her the two threads. She recognizes the threads right away. She shows me my tapestry and says:

'Look, there is a lot of joy and creativity in your tapestry already. These threads will really make it pop and shine even more.' She proceeds to weave both threads making sure that they are intertwined. When she is finished, she adds, *'You will have creative joy and joyful creativity.'* I laugh and thank her.

Urd then shows up and brings out a past tapestry of mine that is surrounded by creativity, but it is darker. I thank her and ask if I could rub her temples. She smiles and nods. When I am finished, she says, *'I see a lot of joy and creativity in your future.'* I finally return to the pool. The three Sisters tell me that, because I have been so kind to them, they will give me a gift. I smile. They allow me to drink from the spring feeding the pool. I approach the water fall and they instruct me to drink only three bubbles and to inhale the water spray. It feels wonderful. I thank them one last time and return.

Check-in with Celeste

I did this journey at a time where I was unable to create anything that I was pleased with. I would start a painting only to cover it with white paint several weeks later. Nothing was working, nothing was inspiring. After this journey, I let the gifts from the Wyrd Sisters sit with me for a while. Then one morning, when I least expected it, I started to draw. Nothing major, but it just started to flow. I picked up the brush and found pure joy in just painting, not for the outcome but for the ability to let go. This was a significant teaching for me.

Self-Healing Journey: Perspectives

*I journey to Grandfather because I am having issues that
keep me awake at night. I usually have no problem sleeping
but I find myself waking up at around 3 am going over an
ongoing problem. I convince myself to go back to sleep, to
let go, but then I start spinning it over and over in my head.
I decide to journey to my guide.*

Celeste (2009)

Grandfather Medicine sits there, patiently waiting for
me to explain my problem. These problems are crystal clear
to me every night as I lie awake at 3 am trying to resolve
them. Yet, as I now sit face to face with Grandfather
Medicine, I have difficulty expressing what I need from
him. My problems suddenly seem so insignificant and I feel
a little ashamed to bother him with such trifle issues. I
stumble on my words for several seconds, blathering on
until I decide to just stop talking.

Grandfather stands up and motions me to do the same.
We stand face to face in silence. Then he sighs and says,
'Shift your eyes slightly to the left, like this.' His whole body
stands perfectly still but his eyes shift almost imperceptibly

to the left and then look forward again. He repeats the motion several times then he encourages me to try it.

I feel a bit silly, thinking he has dismissed my complaints and is now showing me something completely obscure. He holds both of my hands in his and gently prompts me, *'Try it.'*

I take a deep breath and, without moving my head or my body, I shift my gaze slightly to the left and stare forward again. I repeat this several times and am amazed to find that when I shift my gaze, just ever so slightly, the whole world around me changes: the landscape becomes completely different, the air smells different, I could hear different things.

I repeat this shifting gaze over and over again and marvel at how so different the world could be. I start to laugh and ask Grandfather, *'This is so cool, how is this possible? The whole world looks different when I do this one little eye motion.'*

He laughs and says, *'Now imagine what would happen if you moved your entire head.'*

Check-in with Celeste

This journey had a profound impact on me. It was a clear reminder that whatever is going on, no matter how trivial or how significant, the way I react to it is a choice. The story I am making up in my head about what is going on is just that, a story. This story is fed by my beliefs, my insecurities, my ego, my past experiences. Since it is a story, I always have the choice of creating a new story, of choosing to see things differently. Contemplating an experience from various perspectives has allowed me to stay in a state of flow and balance. Now, when I find myself struggling with something, I ask myself: *How can I see this differently? If I were an innocent bystander watching this unfold, what would I see? If I remove myself from myself to witness myself bathing in a river of emotion, what would I see?* This is a great teaching in compassionate detachment.

Self-Healing Journey: Moon Mother

When I feel disconnected or a bit out of sorts, I journey to ask to be nourished energetically.

Celeste (2003)

Healing Journey for Celeste

I sit on the seashore until Moon Mother appears. As she rises and glimmers on the water's surface, water beings appear. They form a circle and dance, swaying to and fro like waves. It is incredibly beautiful, bringing tears to my eyes. They open up the circle and invite me in. I enter the circle and begin swaying, feeling the rhythm of Moon Mother guiding us. As we dance, we go into the ocean farther and farther away from shore. I do not care because dancing this way is so invigorating and so liberating. I stare up at this wonderful Moon Goddess and feel pure love.

Then suddenly, the circle disappears, and I begin to sink into the water. I struggle to keep my head above the waves. I sink deeper and deeper. Giving a final effort, I push myself above the surface and gasp for air. The water beings have returned but they are not helping me. They simply watch me struggle in silence. I start sinking again, this time going deeper than ever before. I finally run out of breath, and know I am drowning. I let my body sink and let everything go. I then slip out of my body and return to the water's surface as a water being. I start dancing and splashing around with the circle. The water beings bring me back to shore and return to the sea. I look up at Moon Mother and thank her. I feel different.

Check-in with Celeste

I have found that journeying with no particular question or problem is such a good way to get fed energetically and to be re-empowered. When I am feeling stuck and a bit down, I journey to an element or animal spirit guide and ask for a teaching. It always makes me feel better.

Self-Healing Journey: The Story of Eagle Brother

One of my first guides and teachers showed up for me as Eagle Brother. He is with me in all journeys and is my protector. I was curious about our bond so I journeyed to him and asked him to tell me his story.

Celeste (2001)

He was a small native boy living in a small village with his tribe. One day, he wandered off into the forest. He got lost and could not find his way back home. He climbed up a tree but could not see his village. He walked up a cliff and still, he could not see his village. He went further and further but he could not find his home. It was getting dark and he was exhausted. He looked around for a place to sleep and found an eagle's nest with two eggs inside. He climbed into the nest and laid down beside the eggs, careful not to disturb them. He fell asleep. That night, when Eagle Mother returned to her nest, she was surprised to find a small human child. She picked him with her huge talons and was about to throw him off the cliff when the child awoke. He begged Eagle Mother for his life explaining that he was lost. Eagle Mother, soon to be a mother herself, felt compassion for this little boy and decided to let him stay in the nest. She raised him as her own with her two eaglets. He learned the way of the eagle, he mastered the language of eagle, and learned how to fly with his brothers.

One day, as he soared high into the sky, he spotted a village down below. Suddenly remembering his human mother and sister, he swooped down to find them. He found them both by the river. He appeared before them and said, *'Mother, I am your lost son! Sister, I am your lost brother!'* His mother and sister cried out. Although they could see him and touch him, they did not believe he was really there. He felt great hurt and his heart ached. He returned to his Eagle Mother and shared his pain. Eagle Mother said that he was more eagle than human now. The young man said he wanted to help his human mother and sister in some way. Eagle Mother told him he could help them by protecting them and guiding them through the path of the Eagle.

So, when Eagle Brother's human mother crossed over to the land of her ancestors, Eagle Brother guided her and showed her the way. And, when his sister decided to become a healer, they made a pact to always be together. They meet in the field between the worlds, Eagle Brother protecting his sister and his sister bringing eagle medicine to the world of humans.

Check-in with Celeste

Certain shamanic teachings tell us not to share the identity of helping guides and teachers. When I initially started working with Eagle Brother, I kept his identity to myself. Then, in one particular journey, Eagle Brother gave me specific instructions on how to honor him in this world. At this time, he also gave me permission to speak about him. He told me that the veil between ordinary and non-ordinary reality is getting thinner, and part of the work is to bring wisdom back in a manifest way for more and more people to be awakened.

Self-Healing Journey: She Came

Help me re-connect with my inner child.
Celeste (2006)

It is a glorious summer day for a walk in the field. The sun caresses my cheeks and a gentle breeze brings the fragrance of buttercups and strawberries to my nose. And then, suddenly, I see her... this wild child playing in the long grass. When she sees me, she runs toward me. I pick her up and smother her face with kisses. She giggles and lets me touch her messed-up golden hair covered in grass and straw. Her face is filthy but her eyes, oh her eyes are like two sparkling jewels. I put her down and we start playing in the field. We make flower necklaces and place them around each other's necks and wrists. We lie down in the tall grass looking up at the blue sky, chewing on clover. We run and sing pretending we are birds. Then, a young girl appears. She is not quite a teenager but shows the sign of pre-pubescence. Her tiny breasts are starting to bulge from her t-shirt, her hair is long and greasy, and she is pale, anemic-like. She is timid and very self-conscious and, although she approaches us, she looks down. The wild child runs to her and takes her hand. She brings this awkward pre-teen to me. I lift her chin and stare into her eyes. There is a lot of intelligence in her eyes but also so much shame and guilt. I sit down and take her in my arms and cradle her. I rock her back and forth as she sobs uncontrollably. I tell her that she is beautiful and that I love her. The wild child hugs her too and whispers she loves her also. We rock to and fro like this until the girl is all cried out. Then, the three of us stand up and we start singing songs and decorating each other's hair with flowers and leaves. We giggle as we sing. We are so happy. Then a young woman shows up. She is standing straight and tall, filled with pride. She wants to join us but does not want to get her dress dirty. We run to her. The wild child messes up her hair and the pre-teen ceremoniously puts a garland around her neck. Then the young woman laughs and kicks off her heels and joins us. Others come that afternoon, many others; and we laugh, and we play, and we hug each other.

As we play in the field, Anandamayi Ma, the Indian saint of perpetual state of divine joy, suddenly appears from the sky. She approaches me and kisses me. Her smile is pure love. I want to follow her wherever she will take me. She makes my whole being vibrate with love. She kisses all of the girls and women in the field, then she flies away. But before she disappears, she blows me a kiss. Suddenly, I am a luminescent being. One at a time each girl starts running toward me. As I open my arms to embrace them, they enter my body and melt into my heart. When my heart is full, I walk back home.

Check-in with Celeste

The intent of this journey was to re-connect with my inner child. I believe this journey was much more than that. I believe this is a classic soul retrieval journey. As Sandra Ingerman points out, *'The soul retrieval process is when a shaman moves into an altered state of consciousness to travel to realities outside of normal perception to retrieve the lost part of the soul. Once the soul is located, the shaman will acknowledge the former pain and gently negotiate the soul's return to the body.'* During this journey, I was given the gift of several lost soul parts: including my wild child and my pre-teen self which allowed for my young professional self to be healed. Soul retrieval can be difficult to explain. Words and rational thought limit us when trying to describe such a profound experience. Sometimes we feel disconnected, and no matter what we do—meditate, read inspiring passages, think positive thoughts—we feel as if we are suffering from a constant slow leak of energy. We do not feel whole. Soul loss, or a sense of loss of our own light, personal power, or essence leads to imbalance and disharmony in our lives. This sometimes leads to numbness and lack of purpose and meaning. As Sandra Ingerman puts it: *'As people feel more present in their bodies and in the world, they become more conscious of behavior that might be out of balance and disharmonious. When we are numb, we might be aware that things in the world are not right, but we can easily distract ourselves from feeling a need to change. When we are fully "inspirited", there is no place to retreat to and we are more inspired to change our lives.'* Soul retrieval and reconnecting with our own true essence is truly a gift and, for many, allows to move energetic flow in a more positive and purposeful way.

Self-Healing Journey: The Stone and the Feather

Please give me a teaching and guidance about life.
Celeste (2011)

A desert like landscape unfolds before me. There are mounds and mounds of red sand as far as the eye can see. A young native man appears. He is running up and down the mounds without stopping. I sit by a fire pit and just watch him. I finally fall asleep watching the young man running up and down. When I awaken, the young man is sitting in front of me. He looks like a bird man. I ask him if he has a teaching for me. He picks up a huge book and starts leafing through it. He puts it aside and says, *'You have had enough of those teachings.'* He adds, *'Why do you need guidance?'*

I think for a while and reply, *'I want to learn, I want to become better, to become one with all.'*

He says this: *'Yes, but when you get the guidance what you do is put it under a glass, like a rose under a glass. You say: there is my gift, these are my teachings, look how beautiful it is but you do not use it. Use the gift, use it a lot.'*

He then shows me an old leather pouch and tells me that the pouch is his gift. It is old and beaten up. He says that by using one's gift, it makes one appreciate the gift more. Then he smiles and says, *'Oh, I have a teaching for you.'*

He brings out a feather and a stone. He asks me if I know this teaching already. I say I think he will ask me which is stronger, the stone or the feather. He smiles and says, *'No, that is not the teaching. Tell me how these two are the same?'*

I think about this for a while and I am not sure how to answer. He closes his fists and opens them up again. He now holds two stones. He places both stones in a pouch and when he empties the pouch, there are now two feathers. He says,

'They are both the same.'

He puts them together and they become one object. He adds, *'They are the same, just like we are all the same. This is not just a saying: I could be you and you could be me. We are each other.'*

I ask him how I could use this teaching. He thinks about this for a while and adds: *'The stone is your head, and the feather is your heart. You act as if they are different but they are the same. They are not separate. Use them together, as one. You want to help others, listen to them as if you were listening to yourself speak. Watch them as if you were watching yourself. Now that will be a different experience. We are all one.'*

I thank him and then on a whim I ask him if my father is here. To my surprise, he tells me that my father is on the mountain. He offers to take me to him. I take his hand and we jump up and down the dunes. We reach the mountain and climb up. My father is there resting. I greet him, *'Hello Father.'*

He responds, *'Hello Daughter. Come rest your head on my lap. You have had enough teachings for one day.'*

As I rest on his lap, I ask him, *'Father, am I your daughter in flesh and bone only or am I also your spirit daughter?'*

He responds, *'Yes, that is one way of putting it. In all ways we are all one, our relationship is no lesser in body than it is in spirit. Can I say to my finger, the other finger is more me? Can I say to one eye, the other eye belongs more to me? We are all one.'*

Check-in with Celeste

There were so many powerful teachings in this journey that it stayed with me for many weeks afterwards. It was important for me to be reminded that the wisdom I sought did not come from books and that a gift must be used like a well-worn leather pouch. Teachings about wholeness and oneness are recurring themes in my journeys. I liked the way this young man explained it in a simple, straight-forward manner. I was particularly touched by his message to listen to others like I was listening to myself. This practice added a rich layer to my thoughts and feelings about compassion.

Self-Healing Journey: Clashing Rocks

Bring me to the legendary Cyanean Rocks, the Clashing Rocks, for a teaching.

Celeste (2002)

Eagle Brother brings me to the Clashing Rocks. The Rocks loom large before me and make an ear-shattering noise as they clash together rhythmically. Eagle Brother leaves me and says he will come back for me. Left to my own devices, I am trying to figure out a way to get through the rocks without being harmed. Since my mind cannot conceive of a way, I decide to journey to the Spirit of the Rocks. When I reach the Spirit of the Rocks, I ask him if he can let me through unscathed, so that I could go to the Cave of Crystals to obtain some wisdom. I explain that I will use this wisdom to help others. I beg for his compassion. He grumbles and huffs and growls, and finally, after a long pause, he says he will let me through, but only this one time, because I have vowed to use my wisdom to help others.

Suddenly, I am in front of the enormous rocks again and am surprised by the eerie silence. The Rocks have opened up and remain open. I tentatively start to cross, warily looking from side to side at the enormity of the stone. They go up as far as the eye can see. The sheer mass of them sends shivers up my spine as I imagine what it would feel like if they suddenly clashed together again. I hurry through, and just as my footsteps reach onto the other side, I hear a grinding noise and the huge boulders start clashing together again.

I turn my attention to the scene before me. I am surrounded by beautiful, lush gardens and up on a hill there is a large cave. I enter the cave and I am filled with awe by its beauty. The cave is made entirely of crystals. They shine brightly and reflect off each other. It is truly a magical place. A beautiful woman appears before me and tells me she is the Goddess of the Cave. I bow to her and ask her for a teaching so that I could help others. She smiles and retrieves one of the crystals from my pouch and replaces it with one of the crystals in the cave. Before she places it in my pouch, she holds it up and makes it sing. As the crystal starts to sing, all of the crystals in the cave start to sing with her. The Goddess disappears and I am alone in the Cave of Crystals with a new crystal in my hand. I gently place it in my medicine pouch.

When I emerge from the cave, I suddenly remember the Clashing Rocks and know I have to figure out a way to return to Eagle Brother. The Spirit of the Rocks has granted me only one safe passage, so I have to figure out a way to get through. I again journey to the Spirit of the Rocks and thank him for his compassion and ask him if he would allow me to leave unscathed by the Rocks so that I could help people. He gets very angry and says that he has already allowed me to get through once and that once was enough.

He says, *'Why should I let you go? What is so special about you?'* I tell him that I now have the wisdom I need to go help others, and that if he lets me go, I will tell any and all that would ask about the might of the Clashing Rocks and how ominous they are.

He chuckles, saying that everyone already knows about the might of the Clashing Rocks. He does not need me to spread a well-known tale. Thinking quickly, I add, *'But, I will also tell those who seek the Truth that the Spirit of the Rock offers great compassion for those who honor it, and that when rock clashes against rock, beautiful crystals emerge. Let me get through and I will tell the true tale of the Cyanean Rocks.'* The Spirit of the Rocks remains silent and then, suddenly, there is complete silence again as the Rocks open up and remain open. I quickly thank the Spirit and run through as fast as I can. I can see Eagle Brother waiting for me on the other side. And again, as my foot takes its last step beyond the Rocks, a deafening, grinding noise begins again and the mighty Rocks start clashing together.

I share my adventure with Eagle Brother who starts to laugh so hard, tears are streaming down his face. I am a bit upset and ask him what is so funny. He tells me that he could bring me to the Crystal Goddess any time I want without going through the Clashing Rocks. As we return, he says, *'Next time, be clear about your intent.'*

Check-in with Celeste

This journey was assigned to us during one of my many shamanic classes. I find this kind of journey to be both fun

56

and informative. I like to delve into Greek, Norse, or Egyptian mythology and ask my guide to bring me to a famous mythical story or figure to see what unfolds. This journey reminds me of the classic hero's journey, the quest to find a hidden treasure, by overcoming various obstacles. Eagle Brother's teachings held much meaning for me. Our myths and legends have often led us to believe that, in order to find ourselves, a lot of drama and noise is required. Yet, as Eagle Brother suggests, we can also take the inward journey home in a more quiet and subtle manner.

Self-Healing Journey: Teachings

Sometimes I doubt myself and the work I am doing. Give me a teaching to help me find my way.

Celeste (2004)

He let me sit out in the cold for days. Finally, after I have almost given up, he lets me in. He is not upset with me and, strangely, I do not feel upset with him. I feel honored to be in his presence. I apologize for taking up his precious time. I say I just want a teaching from him. He responds: *'Don't apologize to me, apologize to yourself because you have dishonored yourself. You judge what is sacred and what is not. You judge what is good and what is not.'*

I bow my head in understanding. He continues: *'Everything is sacred and nothing is sacred. You are connected to all of it; honor the beauty of it all.'* I nod and marvel at this wisdom, holding it close to my heart. As I am about to thank him, he adds more:

'No human teacher can show the way, or the path, because of their own judgments and mired gaze. Trust your inner wisdom. If you have the patience, I will teach you the path of the compassionate journey, the path to the compassionate realm.'

He pauses and his bright blue eyes stare at me, paralyzing me. Every fiber of my being is tingling. He smiles and asks:

'Are you ready?'

I whisper: *'Yes.'*

Check-in with Celeste

These journeys are always short and to the point. My guides have little patience for my doubt and uncertainty. Yet, no matter how often I go to them and ask for reassurance, they always give me an encouraging and compassionate answer. This teaching is a constant reminder to me about my own patience and compassion for myself and others.

Healing Journey: Pain and Bliss

Why do I sometimes feel this sense of longing and aching?
How can I make it go away?

Celeste (1999)

I climb a tree and then climb up a rope ladder. I reach the clouds where I meet a hooded guide. He points to where I need to go. I enter a fabulous garden. I meet a leprechaun. I ask him if he can help me. He simply giggles and runs away. I keep on walking and approach a dark forest. In the forest I meet an old woman and she brings me to her cave dwelling. She stirs her pots on the stove. There is a man seated at a kitchen table. He is wearing a long beard and a cloak. He turns to me and says:

'Do not worry my child. In order for you to experience, you must ache. Your soul aches to be home among us. You are one of us, but you cannot come home just yet. Your work is not finished. You have so much healing to do. You are so beautiful. Look at you, you have so much to accomplish. Do you know how many thousands are waiting to be healed by you? Come and see.'

He invites me to come to the window and opens it. I see a large group of people holding candles waiting in the dark.

He says: *'You have been here before, you will be here again. Do not be afraid. We are always with you, inside of you.'*

I am now back on the clouds; I am wearing a long robe and I have wings. I start dancing. I am very happy; I see a mirror and look into it. I see my face but I cannot see the wings. Then I see myself as a little girl. The little girl comes out of the mirror and I take her in my arms. We dance together. I ask her to stay with me. She starts to laugh and says, *'I am with you silly.'* Other girls start coming out of me, we giggle and we dance together. One of the little girls gives me a smooth green stone. She says, *'When you need me, rub the stone. I am always with you but sometimes you will forget that I am there.'*

I suddenly see on old native man. I ask him for guidance. He says, *'We are here with you always, to guide you. Do not be afraid. In order to experience you must feel hurt, when you hurt—you grow.'* To show me, he takes out a knife and splits his thumb open. His thumb starts to bleed. He is smiling: *'To you this is shocking. To me, this is bliss. When I bleed, I engage all of my senses: I can smell the blood, I can see the blood, I can taste the blood.'* He sucks his thumb. He adds, *'You must experience all of this world has to offer.'*

We start dancing together. I bow to the four directions: the east, the west, the north, and the south. The old man walks away holding the hand of my little girl. I look at them leaving and then I remember the smooth stone in my hand. I open my hand and rub the stone. The little girl stops and turns around to wave at me. I suddenly feel her all over my body.

Check-in with Celeste

This is was one of my early journeys. At the time I felt I needed to understand why I felt so lonely. This message about the illusion of separateness has been a beautiful reminder, especially when life brings sadness, pain, and suffering. This teaching was significant in my awakening. I began to fully engage in my sensory experiences while simultaneously witnessing this experience. I began to better understand this illusion of separateness that generates pain and suffering, and began to deepen and expand my non-dual awareness in all aspects of my life.

Healing Journeys

These are journeys I have done on behalf of clients. I usually get an email or a phone call requesting a healing. Before I do any healing journey, I meet with the client by phone or in person to get to know them a bit and to obtain their written permission to do a diagnostic journey. Sometimes, I find that, although a client may think he or she knows what he or she needs, my guides provide different information. Sometimes, a client feels or senses a symptom but my guides see the source of the pain and suffering. Therefore, I always do a diagnostic journey first to see what my guides are seeing for a client. Then, I share this diagnostic journey with the client and if and when he or she is ready, the healing journey process begins.

Journey for Marion: Words

'I am in a rut; I feel so tired all of the time. I feel like my life is going nowhere. I am doing daily positive affirmations, I try to meditate, I send love, but it only helps for a while. It feels like I have a slow leak or something. Whenever I start something new, like a job or a project, it goes well, for a while, and then it all starts to fall apart, then my life becomes a shit storm again. I feel ugly and useless.'

Marion (email June 2007)

Diagnostic Journey for Marion

I journey to Crone and ask her to see Marion. Crone gives me a spoonful of a potion she is brewing on her stove. This, she says, will make me invisible. She puts on her black cloak and we venture out into the night. She walks swiftly into the forest. I have a hard time keeping up with her. She then turns and places a gnarled finger on her lips, reminding me to be very quiet. She then cuts a slit into the air and we enter into a different space and time. We find ourselves in a kitchen. There is a small child sitting and looking up at a group of women, some standing, some sitting. There is a large cloud of house flies swarming around the child. As the women talk, more and more flies come out of their mouths. There are so many flies that it is hard to see the child. The child simply keeps her mouth shut for fear of swallowing a fly and stares at the women in the room. I ask Crone what this means. She tells me that the child is Marion and she is trapped there. I ask if we can help. She says yes. I thank her and we return.

After I shared this diagnostic journey with Marion, she tells me that this resonates deeply with her. As she read the journey, she was reminded of her childhood and her relationship with her mother. As an only child, Marion was the focus of a lot of attention. However, her mother was a consummate perfectionist, and as a result, hard to please. Marion felt she could never really measure up. She thought she had "let go" of her mother's grasp years ago in therapy. She can see how her feelings of inadequacy and her perpetual "bad luck" may be related to her childhood.

Healing Journey for Marion

I return to Crone and ask her if we can help Marion. She gives me a potion so that I could be invisible. She then gives me a burlap bag and tells me to hang on to it. We walk into the forest and re-enter the portal. We are again in a room where Marion is sitting there as a young 5-year-old girl. There are a lot of women around her, judging her and telling her how she must be. The words are sticking to her and as the words are accumulating on her tiny body, her shoulders are getting heavier and heavier. The heavier they get, the more Marion bends over, and the more she bends over, the more they tell her to straighten up. She is very quiet.

Crone makes a translucent cocoon around Marion. The words can no longer stick to her. Crone then grabs all of the words and the energy connected to them and she tells me to open up my bag. She shoves everything into the bag and tells me to close it up. She then returns to the women and creates light energy around them. Crone and I hold hands and we start glowing. The women are feeling blessed and healed. They too are glowing. They suddenly truly see each other for the first time and start hugging each other saying sister, mother, daughter.

We then return to Marion and remove the cocoon. She starts to speak to the women and they are in awe of her, seeing her for the first time. We surround Marion with healing energy.

We come back through the portal and Crone makes a huge bonfire. She fills a pot with water and places it on the fire. She tells me to place the bag in the boiling water without opening it. When the water has boiled off, she flips the contents of the pot into the fire. When the fire is all burned out, she gathers up the burnt-up ashes in the pot and brings them to a field where she buries the ashes. As soon as she is finished, a small flower starts growing from the ashes. She smiles and tells me she always likes to see the healing. We start walking back, and before we leave the field, I turn around one last time to look at the flower. The field is now filled with thousands of flowers. It is beautiful. Crone looks at my face and smiles.

Check-in with Marion

Several days after the healing journey, I again meet with Marion. She tells me that she did not feel anything while I was doing the journey but the last few days have been different for her. She feels something shifting but she is not sure what.

A month after the healing journey, Marion sends me this email: *'Hello Celeste. I have been meaning to contact you but things are really busy around here these days. Then last night, I was looking for something and I came across the journey you did for me. As I read it over and over again, I started to cry. Since you have journeyed for me, I feel lighter. It's hard to explain but I do not feel this heavy weight or cloud over my head. I have started a new job (will have to tell you all about it) and I am using my voice for the first time in a long time. I speak up and lo and behold, the world does not come crashing down. Anyways, I am rambling but thanks for all of your help. Not sure what happened, but it does not matter.'*

Marion (email July 2007)

Journey for Linda: Gardening

'I am unsure if you can help or what would need to be done. I had mentioned that I fell in February and still have some of the symptoms. I felt I was starting to feel somewhat better. Very slow process. However, on Friday, I am not sure how this happened. I missed a step and lost my balance. I fell and hit my face on the countertop. It was a very hard fall. Friday, I couldn't sleep since if I laid on one side, my face hurt and on the other side my back hurt. I am afraid, I may have given myself another concussion since the symptoms have returned. I am not sure if it is something you can help me with.'

Linda (2018)

Diagnostic Journey for Linda

I journey to Grandfather Medicine and ask him if we could see Linda. I follow him to a field where Linda is tending a beautiful garden. It is fenced in by an old wooden fence. There is a gate but it is left open. Linda works in the garden, smiling. People come in and out of the garden to help her, mostly women and children. I then notice two other small gardens not far from this main garden. They are much smaller than the large garden and they are also surrounded by a wooden fence. The plants in these gardens are black and wilted. I then notice Linda leaving the large garden and heading towards one of the small gardens. She wants to go work in one of the small gardens. When she tries to enter, a male energy (dark and fuzzy) prevents her from going in. Linda does not challenge him but she is very sad. She then tries to go in a second small garden, but she is blocked again by the same dark energy. Inside this second garden there is a young girl, small and dirty, sitting and waiting in the tall weeds. Linda turns around and returns to the large garden and smiles again. I notice that her energetic field is misaligned—I can see the body of Linda working in the garden but her energetic field is slightly beside her, a bit outside of her body, feeling pulled to the other two gardens. Every once in a while, Linda gathers up her energy and tries to pull it in, but the energy keeps on slipping out.

After sharing the diagnostic journey with Linda, she informs me that, about a year ago, she had left her male partner of seven years. She says it has been a difficult year, missing work because of her concussion and deciding to leave her partner.

1st Healing Journey for Linda

I journey to Grandfather Medicine and ask him if we could help Linda. We return to the community garden where Linda is working. She sees Grandfather and invites him into her garden. Grandfather smiles and touches her face with his hand. He then touches some of the energy that is beside Linda and gently moves it inside of her. He touches her head and this makes her shiver. He then leaves the community garden and goes to the dry and black garden where the male energy is blocking the gate. Grandfather greets him and the entity recognizes him. They hug and Grandfather explains to him that this is not his garden and that he needs to move on to his own garden. The man responds that he is not sure how. An elder shows up and takes the male energy by the hand and they walk down a path. After they have left, Grandfather opens the gate and returns to Linda. He asks her if she wants to come into her garden. She says yes but says she is a bit afraid. He walks beside her and when they reach the gate, he motions for her to walk in by herself. Linda hesitates a bit, then she walks into the garden. She relieves herself into the garden and Grandfather says, *'You are marking your territory.'* Linda laughs. Then a group of ancestors show up and bring a bowl of water. Grandfather touches the water and offers it to Linda. Linda drinks from the water and the water pours from every pore in her body, thus watering the garden. They do this over and over again. Finally, they stop and Linda notices a very small plant starting to grow. She removes the dirt and weeds around it and begins to sing to it. It is very fragile but it is growing. The sun shines on it. Then other little plants start to grow. Then the grandmothers come into the garden being careful not to step on the new growth. They blow energy in the garden and leave little faeries all over. The faeries flitter round and round nourishing the garden. Grandfather then asks Linda if she is ready to visit the other garden. Linda nods. They walk together to the other garden where the little girl is sitting. When Linda crosses the gate, she immediately lies down on the ground. A circle of white clad women enters the garden and makes a circle around Linda's body. Grandfather starts to do work on Linda's throat and stomach area. As he works Linda starts to vomit and vomit. The women capture the vomit in bags which they carry out. Finally, when Grandfather is all done, Linda sits up. She is very weak. The little girl then comes and sits on Linda's lap. Linda rocks her back and forth. They sit like that for a while. Then Linda asks the little girl if she wants to help her plant her garden. The little girl nods. Linda goes to Grandfather and asks him where she can get some seeds. Grandfather points at the little girl. Linda asks her if she has any seeds. The little girl opens her mouth and shows a few seeds on her tongue. Linda takes the seeds and plants them in the ground. They plant the whole garden this way. The little girl opens her mouth, and Linda plants the seed. Then the elders make a line to a well drawing a pail of water. When the pail reaches Linda, she waters the garden. This relay work goes on for a while. Then Linda says she wants to check on the other garden and asks the little girl if she wants to come with her. The little girl says, *'Not yet, but soon.'* So, Linda goes back and forth between both gardens making sure they are thriving. Grandfather says that our work is done for now. I thank him and return.

2nd Healing Journey for Linda

I return with Grandfather Medicine to the garden. Linda is there with the little girl and they are tending the little girl's garden. Linda then walks to her own garden and the plants are thriving. They are now almost as tall as Linda. She is pleased. She then returns to the little girl and asks her if she wants to come and visit Linda's garden. The little girl hesitates. Linda says, *'I will carry you.'* So, the little girl says yes. Linda picks up the little girl and they make their way to the garden.

When they reach Linda's garden, the little girl is in awe of it and says, *'I will sing to your garden.'* So, the little girl starts to sing to the garden and the plants sway to her crystal-clear voice. The little girl then invites Linda to sing to her little garden. So, they return to the little girl's garden and Linda says she has not sung like that in a long time and is not sure if she knows how. The little girl rubs her own throat and then rubs Linda's throat. She does this several times. Linda tries to sing but she is having a hard time. She then feels a huge lump in her throat and a huge bull frog comes out. Surprised, they both look at the frog and then they start to laugh. Linda tries again, and this time, all kinds of bugs like grasshoppers, butterflies, fireflies start to come out and they play around in the garden. The little girl really likes that. Linda tries to sing again, and this time, it sounds like a deep toning, very soft at first and then stronger and louder. She starts to sing and the plants start to sway. The little girl claps her hands in delight.

Then, Linda asks the little girl if she wants to go to the community garden. The little girl replies *'No, not yet, we need to tend our gardens first.'* Then the little girl suggests that they make a path connecting both gardens. They create a dirt path between the gardens and the little girl whispers into Linda's ear, *'Soon our two gardens will be one.'* She then looks at Linda and gives her a big smile. As I am about to leave, I notice a vine starting to creep along the path from Linda's garden to the little girl's garden.

Check-in with Linda

After the healing journey, Linda informs me that she had an uninterrupted night's sleep, something she had not experienced in over a year. She tells me that she feels lighter and that her headaches are subsiding. We work together on how she can nurture her inner child and how she can be gentler and patient with herself. She finds that she has now more clarity around her choices and who she is meant to be.

Journey for Denise: Dancing

'I am writing this email to you to ask you for help. I understand the concept of how we lose pieces of ourselves through life trauma. I have felt for a long while that I am not whole, but swimming in circles, wanting to move forward, but knowing something is missing or lost. Negative people drain my energy. I find as time goes on, I cannot be around them, including people I work with. My husband has asked me if I am depressed… and I am not. I am sure it is far deeper than that. I am not a sad person; I always look for the positive in everything.

Can you help me?'

Denise (2016)

Diagnostic Journey for Denise

I journey to Grandfather and ask him if we could see Denise. He nods and brings me into a cave. Denise is lying down on the ground and Grandfather starts looking at her energy. He shows me that there is tremendous amount of weight in her belly area. There is also a large weight surrounding her heart and there is a cord linking the weight around her heart to the weight in the stomach area. Grandfather says that it is very difficult to move with all of this weight. I ask him to show me. We are now in a field area and Denise is standing beside a cage. Inside the cage is a man and woman, both holding each other. There is a cord wrapped up around Denise's stomach and heart. The other end of the cord is connected to the man and the woman inside the cage. Denise starts to dance and moves around. She fills up with light and brightness (butterflies, fairies, and soft light surround her). She feels really good for a while, but then the "gathered up energy" enters the cord and is "sucked up" by the man and the woman in the cage. Denise does this over and over again and every time her energy is depleted, she falls on her knees completely drained and tired. She then gets up and starts dancing again. I also notice that when she dances and gathers up energy, other energies approach her and try to get some of the energy she is gathering. She has great difficulty holding the energy for herself. I ask Grandfather, what we can do. He says, *'It does not matter how much she dances, and how much energy she gathers up, she will not be able to sustain it until we cut the cord from the cage. Then we can help her fill herself up with her own essence. Then she will no longer have to give her energy to others.'* I thank him and come back.

After she has read the diagnostic journey, Denise tells me she cried and cried. She says that this journey captured exactly how she felt. For the first time in a long time, she says, she feels hopeful.

Healing Journey for Denise

Grandfather and I go searching for Denise. After days and days of walking we finally find her trapped in a cage. Grandfather approaches her and whispers something in her ear. She nods and then Grandfather gently blows in her face. Denise is transformed into a small bird. She hops on Grandfather's finger and he gently removes her from the cage. Then Denise-bird sits on my shoulder and Grandfather and I fly higher and higher and farther and farther away, like eagles. We finally land in a spot where there is a group of indigenous women. Denise returns to her human form and the women start cleansing her feet and her whole body. They wash her and cover her entire body with a healing salve. One woman combs out her long hair. Denise is very relaxed. Then, they start painting a whole bunch of symbols on her body starting with her face. There are geometric shapes, and spirals—her whole body becoming covered in tattoos. They move back and form a circle around Denise. Grandfather tells Denise to dance the symbols. Denise says she is not sure how. Grandfather says, *'Just start moving.'* So, she does. She starts dancing this beautiful dance. She becomes a swirl of motion. She swirls around for quite a while until she is so fatigued, she drops to the floor. One of the indigenous women brings her water to drink. Grandfather says, *'She is not finished dancing.'* So, Denise starts moving again, but this time it is a more forceful dance, like an angry warrior dance. She dances "angrily". The skies become dark and a huge thunderstorm begins. The rain pours down in sheets, and lightning, thunder, and wind surround us. Denise dances throughout the violent weather. She dances and dances until she becomes so tired, she drops to the floor again. Then the thunderstorm stops. A woman gives her more water. Grandfather says again, *'She is not finished dancing.'* So, Denise begins to dance again. This time, a gentle breeze comes up and Denise dances a slow flittering dance, like a little bird. It is gentle and soft and beautiful. As she dances, I notice the symbols on her body are fading away. She dances like this for quite a while and then she stops and smiles. The women gather around her and hug her. Denise flies down to the river and sits there. She marvels at what she sees.

She says, *'This is amazing, when I breathe in, I breathe in the trees, and they feel so good. When I breathe in, I feel the love of the river. It's so amazing.'* She just sits there breathing in the love and beauty of Mother Nature. Grandfather gathers up all of the energy and love Denise is feeling and blow it into her eyes, ears, mouth, and top of her head. Lastly, he takes a deep breath and blows it into her heart.

Check-in with Denise

'Hope this email finds you well. I am very well and adjusting to being "whole." The void that I have felt for so many years seems to be full of joy and love. The last 2 weeks have been very positive for me. My husband says my eyes have that "sparkle" and I have laughed more in the last couple of weeks than I have in years. I am calmer and learning to keep my energies for myself (...) I think I may

learn to journey in the future for this guidance regarding these issues.

Have a great weekend!'

Denise (2018)

Healing Journey for Celia: Making Bubbles

I am in desperate need for you to do a journey on my behalf. I've been struggling with inner turmoil for several months now and I'm feeling fragmented, lost. Small things that used to make my heart soar no longer do so. I feel joyless and in pain. My husband is still my rock but it's all taking a toll on him too. Everything feels dark, cheerless, and frightening. I feel I'm surrounded by pain, death, lack of hope—lack of joy that used to come so easily to me from the smallest places. I feel useless. And I'm so sorry. Can you please help?

Celia (2018)

Diagnostic Journey for Celia

Grandmother brings me to a large beach by the ocean. Celia is running around frantically along the shore picking up various "pieces" of herself. There are pieces scattered all over the beach. She retrieves a piece and tries to hold it in her arms but when she scoops down to pick up one piece, another piece falls. She is very discouraged and cries a lot. I then see a woman sitting quietly on a rock above the beach watching all of this very calmly. Grandmother says that Celia is stuck in a world of separateness, in the illusion of separateness. I then notice that Celia has succeeded in gathering most of her parts, but then, a huge wave comes crashing down on the shore and she falls back, dropping all of the pieces. Some of the pieces are lost in the ocean with the receding wave. Celia is very frustrated and cries helplessly. She then gets up and tries to collect the pieces again. This pattern of picking pieces and the wave crashing down repeats itself over and over again.

After the diagnostic journey, Celia sends me this e-mail: *'The diagnostic journey you have done clearly details for me the path I am on right now. I've been frantically picking the various pieces of myself and dropping the previous piece when I found the next. Every facet of my life feels like this right now. I've been trying so hard—and failing quite well (!)—to hold it all together. I've lost all my connections with the talismans of my heart and soul. It's left me feeling so fragmented that I'm not able to do anything in my day to day life well. I am ready for a healing session. Thank you from all my heart for the diagnostic journey you completed for me this morning. I look forward to the next step—I need to work on healing.'*

Celia (2018)

Healing Journey for Celia

I return with Grandmother to the beach where Celia is still gathering all the pieces. Grandmother takes a deep breath and then lets it out. Her breath makes the water of the ocean recede. But then, after a few seconds, a huge wave comes crashing down on the beach and it takes all of Celia's pieces away. Celia is devastated and starts to cry uncontrollably. Grandmother then approaches her. Celia sees Grandmother before her but cannot stop crying. She says she has lost everything. Grandmother smiles at her and says, *'Then who is speaking with me now?'* Celia seems confused. Grandmother then creates a bubble around Celia and she lifts it up into the air, like a large bubble of soap. Grandmother then brings Celia in her bubble into a room where she sits down in front of Celia and tells her that the image on the beach is just an image she has created of herself: it is an illusion, like the bubble she is in now. Grandmother then starts making other bubbles and invites Celia to enter into different bubbles. Celia starts floating around from bubble to bubble. When one bubble pops, she enters into another bubble. She finds this funny but also a bit distressing. Grandmother says she should try making bubbles herself. Celia says she does not know how. Grandmother then brings Celia a book filled with blank pages and gives her some coloring crayons. She tells her to draw an image of what a good bubble would look like. At first Celia starts to draw an image but then she says she has never been shown how to draw an image of a good bubble. She does not know what it would look like if she were in a "good" bubble. Grandmother touches Celia's eyes and the top of her head and says, *'Just draw, don't judge. Just draw.'*

So, she starts making various shapes on the paper, using different colors. After a while she stops and says, *'It's just a bunch of random shapes, just pieces here and there, it's not really anything.'* Then Grandmother takes the paper and posts it on the wall. As Celia sees her fragments from a distance, she realizes that she has created a beautiful mandala. She starts to cry because it is so beautiful. Grandmother tells her to go inside her mandala. She does, and she explores all of the various colors: reds, and blues, pinks, yellows, and oranges. She explores all of the various shapes and their colors and she feels different emotions as she explores. She tells Grandmother that if she did not know this was a beautiful mandala, she would think it was just random colors. She then emerges from the mandala.

Grandmother stares into Celia's eyes and says, *'You can create this and live this anytime. There is only love: everything you are and everything you do is love. Love is beautiful, it is inherently beautiful, there is no ugliness or imperfection, just beautiful love, that is you. When we see something different than love, it is a choice we make.'*

Celia thanks Grandmother. She replies that she would have to work on this. So, Grandmother brings her into a room filled with children drawing pictures. She approaches one of them and asks her what she is drawing. The child says that she is drawing a princess on a horse slaying a dragon. When Celia looks at the paper, all she sees are a few scribbles.

Grandmother smiles and says, *'Remember how to see again. This little girl is seeing a beautiful princess slaying a dragon. You choose to see scribbles.'*

Check-in with Celia

After the journey, Celia sent me this email: *'I felt a change/shift while you went on the healing journey for me.*

I honestly did. My head felt light, my step felt light—almost floating. While you journeyed, I slowly and carefully shelled green peas from our garden. Carefully split each pod open and marveled at the little peas inside. I don't often look at simple things like this anymore. I view most things so darkly as if they're a threat. It's where my fear of everything is born. I've carefully read each word you wrote as if I was shelling those words like peas. I still feel calm. I know there is more to what you've so kindly sent to me—what I seem to be doing right now is welcoming each phrase and seeing where it might take me. I found Grandmother's presence to be soothing. She is very powerful. Over the next few days I will let this healing journey follow its course with my eyes no longer closed to possibilities of finding again my true spirit. Even how I've written these words is different. I need to allow myself to accept healing. There are wounds that I need to stitch closed with care and knowledge of why.'

Celia (2018)

Healing Journey for Maria: Who is This?

'I am wondering if you are still making time to journey on behalf of others? I have recently been struggling with so much old shadow ideas of myself, deep rooted seeds I thought (hoped) were healed. It's not often I feel like I need help but, I'm feeling a bit suffocated. Can you journey for me?'

Maria (2017)

Diagnostic Journey for Maria

I go to my guides and ask them about Maria. We walk into a large field. It is summer and the field is filled with wild flowers. Maria is in the field by herself and she is picking flowers. When she has picked a bouquet, she returns to a little cabin and places the flowers in a glass jar. She then looks outside the window and returns in the field to pick more flowers. She then returns to the cabin and places this new bouquet of wild flowers in another jar. I then notice that there are hundreds of bouquets of flowers in the cabin. They are everywhere. Some flowers are still fresh but many are wilted and some black. Maria sits for a bit in the cabin, she sighs and then returns to the field to pick more flowers. I ask my guide what is going on and if we can help her. He says, *'She is trying to pick all of the flowers, but she is finding the task tiring and never ending.'* I ask what we could do. He says, *'She is blinded right now. She sees the world in a certain way and we need to help her change how she sees the world. She wants to capture the beauty of the flowers and make it her own, yet she does not see that the beauty is already around her. She does not need to capture it. She is yearning for something but repeats the same thing in search of herself.'* I ask if we can help. He says, *'Yes, we can help if she wants to leave this place. She may not be ready yet.'*

After I send this diagnostic journey to Maria, she sends me this email: *'Thank you. This journey is not what I expected but makes absolute sense. I have been given this scenario by healers many times throughout my life. I am absolutely ready to heal. I would be honored if you would do a healing for me.'*

Maria (2017)

Healing Journey for Maria

We sit on a cliff for a while overlooking what seems to be a huge valley, like the Grand Canyon. Grandfather gets up and draws a large circle in the sand with his staff. He starts making geometric shapes dividing the circle in sections. He does this for a while. Then he places Maria in the middle of the circle. He makes intricate gestures with his hands and the circle starts to burn. Flames are coming from the various geometric shapes and from the outside perimeter of the circle. All of a sudden, the flames come in closer and closer until they reach Maria and she burns. The essence of Maria is released and watches the burning figure with us. Grandfather asks her, *'Who is burning?'*

Maria responds, *'Maria.'*

My guide asks, *'Then who are you?'*

Maria responds, *'Maria.'*

He does not say anything but leads us to a river with very fast rapids. He pushes Maria into the river. She tries to swim but she eventually drowns. The essence of Maria watches this with us on the shore. Grandfather asks her *'Who drowned?'*

Maria responds, *'Maria.'*

'Then who are you?' he asks.

She replies, *'I am also Maria.'*

We then walk in the desert for a while. Suddenly, there is a deafening rumble. A herd of buffalo is charging toward us. We get out of the way but Maria is trampled. The essence of Maria watches this unfold before us. Grandfather asks her, *'Who is that?'* pointing to the broken body.

This time Maria says, *'An empty shell.'*

Grandfather nods and smiles. He says, *'Yes, now you understand. Who are you then?'* The essence of Maria starts pulsating and dancing, and everything around us just blows up and the whole place becomes an oasis. It is beautiful to watch. The essence of Maria is radiating. She pulsates for a while and then returns to her Maria body form. Grandfather tells her, *'Stop playing this game. You know this. You have always known this. Do not confuse the shell with who you need to be. If the shell does not serve you in the way it needs to, remove yourself and become something different. You know this. Stop this silliness.'* He watches her for a while scolding her with his eyes. Then he has a huge smile and takes her face in his hands and repeats, *'You know this beautiful one.'*

Check-in with Maria

I did not get any response from Maria after this journey. I am not sure how she received the journey.

Healing Journey for Melissa: Patterns

'I am having a really hard time. My friend told me about the work you do. I feel I am stuck. I used to be a happy and content person but I am depressed. My husband and I moved to a new town a few years ago and I am feeling so lonely. I am no longer myself. I am not sure what is going on. Even my mother is noticing that I am stuck and drawn into myself. Can we talk about this to see how you can help?'

Melissa (2017)

Diagnostic Journey for Melissa

Grandfather and I walk for a long time in a desert-like place. We arrive at a ridge overlooking a valley below. We walk down into the valley and there, we see a young girl playing with ducks and geese inside a pen. She seems to be quite content and she is very quiet. She does not notice anything around her. There is not much around her except for this pen and the birds. She seems to be focused on taking care of them. We then walk back up into the hills and I notice a cave. Grandfather and I enter the cave. Inside, we see Melissa looking out at the little girl in the valley through a hole in the cave wall. She stands on her tip toes so she can get a better view of the valley. After a while, she steps down and starts walking into the cave. She walks very slowly along the wall of the cave, her back to the wall and her hands feeling her way along. The cave is well lit, but she is very careful not to step into the middle of the cave for some reason. She then arrives at an opening inside the cave where there is a series of strings on the ground forming a number of geometric patterns. It looks like a spider web but more intricate. Melissa proceeds to step into the spaces between the strings, being careful not to touch the strings. If she accidentally touches one of the strings, she goes back and starts all over again. When she finally succeeds and gets to the other side of the cave opening, she walks to a wall and stands there facing the wall. She stands there motionless for quite some time. Then, all of a sudden, it seems like she wakes up or she hears something and she makes her way back through the string pattern, walks carefully along the cave wall and reaches the hole to peer out at the little girl in the valley. She does this over and over again. I ask Grandfather what is going on and what we can do to help. He says, *'She is stuck in a pattern. If we break the pattern, she can be freed from this and return to the open field.'* I ask him for his assistance in doing this.

After this diagnostic journey, Melissa and I talked a lot on the phone. She felt scared and felt she needed to sort out what this journey was telling her. It resonated deeply with her and she felt very emotional. She gave permission for a healing journey several weeks later.

1st Healing Journey for Melissa

We return to the cave where Melissa is now standing facing the cave wall. Grandfather walks the same path she does, walking through the intricate patterns to finally reach her. He asks her if she wants to come with him. She says she cannot because she cannot break the pattern. Grandfather remains silent and returns to the entrance of the cave. After a while, Melissa leaves the wall and starts coming through the web-like pattern, careful not to touch the strings. She then reaches the cave opening and stares at the young girl in the pen in the field. Grandfather approaches her again and shows her that she can avoid the ordeal of walking along the edge by simply going down some stone stairs. And sure enough, stone stairs appear. Melissa is surprised by this, saying she has never noticed those stairs before. Grandfather points out that she can get through the pattern quicker and then to the wall and then back again. Melissa thinks this makes sense and runs down the stairs. She seems pleased. She does this several times. Then Grandfather says he can show her an easier way to see the little girl. Melissa is hesitant but asks how. He points upwards and he shows her an opening in the cave ceiling. She seems a bit skeptical, but Grandfather tells her he can show her how to go through. She replies that she is afraid because if she breaks the pattern something bad might happen. He tells her that he will make sure that nothing bad happens, pointing out that nothing bad had happened when she used the stairs. This seems to convince Melissa and she follows Grandfather outside of the cave. When she emerges, it is nighttime and the sky is filled with stars. Melissa takes large gulps of fresh air as if she is breathing for the first time. She seems to like the feeling, but she keeps on saying that she is afraid and that she is not supposed to do this. She lies down on the ground and watches the night sky in silence. Finally, the sun comes up and Grandfather encourages her to walk down towards the field. Melissa wants to, but she is afraid. Grandfather says he will help her. So she slowly and tentatively walks down toward the field. When she reaches the tall grass, something is holding her back. Grandfather then shows me that hooks are attached to her stomach and to the back of her neck. He approaches those areas and blows on them and the hooks remove themselves and return to the cave. Melissa starts to tremble uncontrollably and collapses. A group of little girls show up and start massaging the areas where the hooks had been. They are like little faeries flying around her. This makes Melissa laugh. They tell her to come with them. Melissa follows. They bring her to a place that they call the crying room and show her how to cry. So, they cry and cry for quite a while. Then they bring her to a place they call the laughing room and show her how to laugh. So, they laugh and laugh. Melissa says she already knew how to do this. They reply, *'No, not really. You have forgotten.'* So, they leave and play in the field laughing and giggling. Then they take Melissa's hand and bring her near the little girl in the penned-up area. They encourage Melissa to enter the pen. She slowly enters and greets the little girl. The little girl says hi, but she is very serious. Melissa asks her what she is doing there. The little girl replies, *'I have to stay here to keep watch.'*

Melissa asks, *'To keep watch on what?'* The little girl says that she does not remember but that it is very important and that she needs to do it otherwise something bad will happen. Melissa tells her, *'I thought that too, but you do not have to anymore. Did you want to play with me?'*

The little girl says, *'I don't know how.'* So, Melissa invites the little faeries to come in and they start playing with Melissa and the little girl. They laugh, and giggle, and cry and laugh again. They make flower wreaths. Finally, Melissa invites the little girl to leave the pen area. The little girl agrees. Melissa picks her up and carries her to a river. They both sit side by side soaking their feet in the healing river. They seem to be quite content. Grandfather smiles and says our work is done.

2nd Healing Journey for Melissa

I return to see Grandfather and ask him if we could check in on Melissa. He nods and we return to the river. Melissa is there with the young girl. They are still sitting in the water and they are combing each other's hair. Melissa is talking quietly to the young girl. The young girl turns to Melissa and says: *'Empty your mind and open your heart.'* Melissa nods but seems a bit confused and just keeps on talking. The young girl brings her fingers to Melissa's mouth and says, *'Shhhh, empty your mind and open your heart.'* Then the little girl adds, *'Come here and let me help you.'* She takes Melissa's head into her hands and pulls it down gently toward the water. She then opens up Melissa's head and shakes the head. A whole bunch of stuff comes out and falls into the water. It is not dark or bad, it is just stuff. The little girl then closes up Melissa's head and blows gently on her forehead. Then she blows on Melissa's heart and it becomes much bigger. The little girl then says, *'Let's go try it out.'* So, they lie down in the grass and the little girl speaks again, *'Look at the sun and connect with the sun with your heart.'*

Melissa lies back and then says, 'Show me how.'
The little girl explains: *'Empty your mind, be quiet and let your heart speak. It knows how.'* They do this for a while. Then, the little girl says, *'Let's do it with a flower.'* They each find a flower and connect with it. Melissa is smiling and beaming.

When they are done Melissa comments, *'I felt like I was the flower, just being and gently dancing with the wind.'*
The little girl responds, *'Yes, that is the heart all right. Now you know how to lead with your heart, not your head.'*

Check-in with Melissa

After the healing journeys, Melissa tells me that she feels these journeys capture her state of mind right now. She explains that she is quite obsessive and she spends a lot of time analyzing things and asking questions. She is delighted to be reunited with the young girl and has started taking daily walks in nature, just connecting. She feels much better and is very light. Several weeks after these journeys, I receive an email from Melissa's mother:

'Hello, I am Melissa's mother. I wanted to tell you that I have had many conversations with Melissa about her experience and her work with you. I watched her struggle for many years with herself, and not knowing how to help her. I am so glad she has found her way.

I see a change in her. Her nature is calmer, she is more loving and patient. Thank you so much for bringing my daughter back.'

Melissa's mother (2017)

Melissa checks in with me on a regular basis. She is feeling much better and is finding a new sense of purpose in her life. She and her husband have decided to move back to their hometown where Melissa feels more supported and more alive.

Healing Journey for Alexandre: Flying

'I feel I am on the cusp of something. I do a lot of meditating and, just when I think I will connect with something significant, I become aware of myself and it slips away from me. I feel a bit trapped and frustrated by the process. Can you help?'

Alexandre (2018)

Diagnostic Journey for Alexandre

I journey to my guides and ask if we could see Alexandre. We walk along a dirt trail until we reach a cliff. Alexandre is sitting there overlooking the panoramic view. He seems content. Then I notice a large bubble surrounding Alexandre. I ask my guide what this means. He says, *'Alexandre enjoys this bubble. He enjoys looking out and observing. If he wishes to move from observing to being and experiencing, we can help him.'* I thank him and return.

After I share this journey with Alexandre, he gives me permission to do a healing journey. He tells me he is ready for the bubble to be burst.

Healing Journey for Alexandre

I journey to my teacher and ask him if we can help Alexandre. We return to the cliff where Alexandre is trapped inside a large bubble. My teacher enters the bubble and speaks to Alexandre. I cannot make out what is being said. He suddenly slaps Alexandre on the cheek, then he blows on his eyes and forehead. He then asks Alexandre if he is ready. Alexandre nods. My teacher makes the bubble roll off the cliff. As it floats in mid-air over the valley below, my teacher removes himself from the bubble and as he does so, the bubble pops. Alexandre is confident at first but then he starts flailing and dropping quickly to the ground. My teacher flies underneath him and supports Alexandre's body. They fly back to the top of the cliff. He encourages Alexandre to try again. Alexandre jumps off and flies for a bit but then he panics when he becomes aware of what he is doing. My teacher flies underneath him again and supports him. At one point, as Alexandre is about to try it again, my teacher says this to him, *'Separate your energetic self from your body. Slip out.'* Alexandre looks at him and then his energetic being slips out. There are now two Alexandres: one in body form, one in energy form. My teacher tells the energetic Alexandre to fly off the cliff first. He does and flies effortlessly. Then, the body Alexandre jumps off and flies to the energetic self and is supported by it. They fly like this for quite some time. Alexandre is smiling from ear to ear.

Alexandre finally returns to the cliff. Before he leaves, my Teacher shares this with him: *'Do not get ahead of yourself; literally, do not get ahead of yourself, your energetic self needs to be aligned with the body self; one is not better than the other, they are the same; do not judge it; you have baby wings, the journey is long; strengthen your baby wings, there is much to learn.'*

Check-in with Alexandre

Alexandre thanks me for the journey. Although he did not feel anything at the time of the journey, he feels like something has shifted within him. He is less analytical and less concerned about things. He feels a renewed sense of energy around his life goals and is ready to move things around.

Healing Journey for Martin: Desert Man

'I am a veteran. I was seriously injured a few years back and I suffer from PTSD. I have had all kinds of treatments and lots of therapy. I was listening to Sandra Ingerman on a live web stream and she was talking about soul loss and soul retrieval. I think I may have suffered soul loss while on duty. I looked on her website and your name came up in the Canadian shamanic practitioners. I would like to discuss how this works with you. Thanks.'

Martin (2018)

Diagnostic Journey for Martin

I journey to Grandfather Medicine and ask him if we could see Martin. We walk around for a bit and then he brings me into a cave. Martin is sitting there by himself. It is dark and cold. Martin is shivering. I notice an opening in the cave where Martin goes to every once in a while, but his leg is attached to something preventing him from getting out of the cave. I look more closely and it is some kind of black rope, like a snake attached around his ankle. I follow it and it leads me to another Martin. This Martin is dark, black, and small, but he is hanging on to the other side of the rope preventing the other Martin from getting out of the cave. I return to the other Martin sitting in the cave and notice that the sun is now shining in through the hole in the ceiling of the cave. Martin approaches the beam of light but he does not want to go too close because it is too bright for him. He prefers staying in the shadow where he can feel the light but not be in it. All of a sudden the scenery changes and Grandfather brings me to a desert-like area. I see Martin walking around aimlessly looking for something. He just walks and walks around. He is very translucent. Then the scenery changes again and I see Martin as a young boy, maybe 8–9 years of age. He is in the bush sitting on a branch of a tree crying. He is all alone and apparently lost. I ask Grandfather what all of this means. He tells me that in order to get Martin out of the cave, we need first to retrieve the man in the desert. Once we have retrieved him, the little boy will come back to Martin and help us get Martin out of the cave.

After this diagnostic, Martin and I discuss what is going with him. He tells me that some parts of the journey resonate for him, but he cannot make sense of other parts. He agrees to proceed with a healing journey.

1st Healing Journey for Martin

I journey to Grandfather Medicine and ask him if we can help Martin. Before we leave Grandfather creates a medicine bundle. He takes a cloth and places various medicinal herbs and powders. He then takes the four corners of the cloth and folds them up and places the bundle in his shirt pocket. We walk in the dark in silence. We reach the desert where the man is walking around aimlessly looking for something. Grandfather approaches him but the man cannot see him. Grandfather then takes out the medicine bundle and sprinkles some of its contents around the man. He makes a large circle around him. Then he hums and sings. The man stops walking around and sits down within the circle that has been made for him. Grandfather tells me that he will be okay there and he is now protected until we come back to get him. We then return to the cave where Martin is standing. Grandfather smudges the entire cave. He then starts drawing geometric shapes in the air. Then, he goes to the small black curled-up Martin and starts humming and singing around him. As he does this, the curled-up Martin starts to move around uncomfortably. The other Martin is standing there not seeming to know what is going on. The dark curled-up Martin gets up and releases the other Martin. The rope that is connecting them loosens up. Grandfather then sits down on the floor of the cave and the curled-up dark Martin comes over to him. Martin now appears to be some kind of dog (like a German shepherd). He is snarling and biting at Grandfather but Grandfather just stares at him. The dog flinches and starts to moan. Grandfather then takes the dog's head and stares right into his eyes. The dog starts to lick Grandfather. Grandfather laughs, pets the dog, and tells him he can go now. The dog becomes light and dissipates. When this happens, Martin sighs a big sigh of relief. Now he can see Grandfather and he smiles at him. Grandfather tells him to come to the light. Martin finds the light of the sun to be too bright at first so he takes his time to get used to it. Grandfather then helps him get out of the cave. Martin is very weak so Grandfather brings him to healing waters. Several healing ancestors show up and start washing Martin with the healing waters. They instruct Martin to soak into one of the healing pools. He does, and as he soaks, black gunk comes out of his body. When all of the black gunk is released, the elders bring Martin to another healing pool of water. He soaks in there for a while and more black stuff comes out of his head. When all of the stuff has finished spilling out of his head, they bring him to another pool. This time, Martin just relaxes. He is very fatigued. Then a wolf shows up and comes to lick Martin's hand. Grandfather tells Martin that the wolf will be his protector now, and that the wolf will always be with him. He says, *'The wolf cares deeply for you and holds your heart. You are one. He will help you heal and will be with you from now on.'* I watch as Martin sits in the healing waters, the wolf resting beside him. Occasionally, the wolf licks Martin's hand. Grandfather tells me that Martin has to stay here and get stronger for a while before we can proceed. He tells me Wolf will stay with him.

2nd Healing Journey for Martin

I journey to Grandfather and ask him if we could check in on Martin. He nods and covers me with a cloak so that I can remain invisible. We go to the desert where a man is sitting there waiting. Grandfather makes himself visible to the man who is shocked that someone can finally see him. The man says, *'I have been lost here for so long, all alone and no one can see me. I am lost in this desert.'* Grandfather gives the man some water and food and asks him if he is ready to leave the desert now. The man nods. Grandfather takes the man on his back and they start to fly. They soar high into the skies until they finally land on a beach. Grandfather creates a bubble around the man and tells him to wait there. The man sits down on the sand and waits, looking out at the water. Grandfather then finds Martin resting on a large boulder and asks him to follow him. When they reach the beach, Martin is surprised to see the man in the bubble. Grandfather invites Martin to enter the bubble. Grandfather then instructs both men to sit back to back. Then he ties their wrists together. Grandfather draws geometric shapes inside the bubble. The desert man suddenly stands up and starts fuming. He is raging, and as he rages, black stuff spews out of his mouth. The dark gooey liquid now pours out from all of his pores. Martin holds the man's wrists the entire time. There is so much black stuff now that we can barely see the two men inside the bubble. I then notice Wolf has joined us and is watching this unfold. When the man has finished storming, Grandfather puts a small tube in his mouth and inserts the other end into the bubble. He starts to suck out the black stuff and spits it into a burlap bag. This takes a long, long time. When all of the black stuff has been removed, Grandfather closes the bag and tells me to bring it somewhere far away and to burn it. When I return, Grandfather bursts the bubble. The desert man is now lying on the ground, totally spent. Some of the gooey stuff is still sticking to him. Martin starts to gently wash all of the black gooey stuff off the man and Wolf helps by licking the goo with his tongue. When the man is cleansed, he looks at Martin and says, *'You are still here man. That is crazy. After all of this shit.'*

Martin says, *'I am not leaving you.'*

The man starts to cry, and cry and cry. He is crying so much that the sand on the beach becomes muddy. His tears join with the water from the ocean and the ocean waves take all of the tears away. When he has finally finished crying, the desert man stands up and Grandfather tells him to dance the dance of the warrior. The man slowly starts to move, then his whole body sways to an ancient rhythm like an indigenous warrior. Martin joins in and they both start to dance. As they dance, I notice that they are starting to merge together. The dance finally stops when Martin and the desert man have totally merged. There is only Martin before us now. An old indigenous man comes forth and paints symbols on Martin's face. He then removes Martin's eyes and gives him new ones. Then he draws geometric shapes on Martin's heart and mumbles, *'Heart of my heart, welcome son. You are one of us now.'* Martin says he wants to honor the old man by washing his feet. A large circle of ancestors chant, sing, and drum as the honor ritual takes place. The old indigenous man then shape-shifts into Wolf.

Grandfather says, *'You are a warrior of the heart now.'*

Martin thanks him and walks down the beach with Wolf by his side.

Check-in with Martin

After this first healing journey, Martin calls me and tells me he has noticed a definite shift. He tells me that when he first came home from his tour of duty, he went to the dog shelter and got himself a big German shepherd. They both needed healing and their relationship was difficult at first. He tells me about two very serendipitous events since the first journey: the first happened at his nearby general store. He was shopping for various things when he noticed a large poster of a wolf. He goes to this store very often and had never noticed a poster of a wolf before. He bought it and put it up on his bedroom wall. The second incident happened when he found out that a group of indigenous people had started to hold healing sweat lodges for the community. Martin has decided to attend and has been going ever since.

After the second healing journey, Martin tells me that his life has changed dramatically. His headaches are not so frequent, he has more energy and more patience with his children. He has been attending his local indigenous circle regularly and he feels very encouraged about his life.

Healing Journey for
Michael: Drowning

'I have heard a lot about soul retrieval. My sister shared what you have done for her. Can you do a soul retrieval for me?'

Michael (2017)

Diagnostic Journey for Michael

I journey to my guides and ask them about Michael. We fly for a long time until we reach what seems to be an ocean beach. Michael is standing on the beach looking toward the sea. He is walking back and forth searching for something on the horizon. There is a dock there and he walks to the end of the dock. There are a few large stones sticking out of the water, making a path into the sea. Michael jumps from the dock to the first stone and tries to keep his balance. He then jumps to the second stone. When he reaches the third stone, a huge wave appears and makes him fall into the water. Michael is drowning in the water but he manages to swim back to shore. He then starts working hard at throwing large stones in the water to make the path more solid. He tries again to jump across the stone path, but every time he tries to get farther a huge wave appears and pushes him off. He does this several times but he is very exhausted. I notice an island far away where there is a little boy watching and waiting. I ask Grandfather if we can help. He shows me that Michael is out of balance. He shows me small stones located in Michael's throat and larger ones in his belly. He also says that Michael's right side is heavier than his left side thus making him out of balance. Although Michael tries very hard to reach the young boy on the island, he loses his balance and falls. Grandfather adds that although Michael is trying to make the path more solid, it is not the path that is out of balance but Michael himself.

After I share this journey with Michael, he informs me that when he was a young boy of about 9 years, an incident occurred with his family. His brother, his brother-in-law, and he went to the ocean beach to relax and play in the water. His sister did not come because she was very pregnant with her first child. Unexpectedly, a large wave came in that afternoon and the three of them were swept away by the under tow. Michael almost drowned that day but his brother saved him. Unfortunately, his brother-in-law did not survive. That event changed him and his family that day. He felt that a piece of himself was still there. He asked me to do a healing journey.

Healing Journey for Michael

Grandfather and I return to the beach. Grandfather walks on the shore and makes himself visible to Michael. He tells Michael that he can help him. He asks Michael if

106

he wants to be helped. Michael says yes. Grandfather tells Michael to follow him. They walk for quite a while down the beach. Then a group of women dressed in white robes show up. Grandfather and Michael follow the women up into caves. They enter the caves filled with crystals. Grandfather tells Michael to lie down on a stone table. Grandfather then starts to hum and makes geometric patterns in the air with his hands. He gently opens up Michael's throat and removes the stone that is blocking his throat. He rubs the area gently and fills it with a crystal. He then pushes against Michael's forehead and places a crystal there. Then he opens up Michael's stomach area and removes all of the stones. He places the stones in a bag and closes up the bag. He then sucks up the poison in the stomach area and spits it in the bag. When this is done the women take the bag and bring it somewhere outside of the cave. Then they return and help Grandfather fill Michael's stomach area with flowers and healing ointments. They rub the inside of the stomach until it is glowing. Grandfather then removes the stones from Michael's right side. He places them in a separate bag and, again, the women take the bag away. He fills Michael up with healing ointment and crystals. He then tells Michael to sit up. Michael is smiling but is very fatigued. The women give him sips of healing water to drink. When Michael has gathered his strength, Grandfather tells him it is time to return to the beach to go find the boy on the island. Michael says he does not know how to cross. Grandfather shows him how he can just skip across the stones and fly up when the waves show up. So they both go down the stone path and when a wave comes up, Michael jumps. They do this for a while and then

Grandfather just makes the waves go right over them so that there is some kind of water tunnel all around them. They finally reach the island and the young boy is surprised to see Michael. They hug and Michael walks along the beach with the boy. After they have walked for a while, Grandfather says it is time to go. Michael asks the boy if he wants to come with him. The boy says, *'Yes but I am scared.'*

Michael responds, *'Do not be afraid, I am here now to protect you. I will always protect you.'*

So the boy jumps on Michael's back and Michael carries him across the water tunnel. The boy is amazed to be able to cross this way. When they reach the shore, the boy is really excited saying, *'I have waited so long for this.'* Michael and the boy play in the sand—they skip stones on the water, they run up and down the beach and just lie in the sand laughing. They are really happy to be together. At one point, they start dancing together, and the ancestors are forming a circle around them.

The ancestors say, *'We are healed too.'*

Check-in with Michael

Several weeks after the healing journey, I re-connect with Michael. He tells me how different he feels. He says he is happier, not so depressed. He feels like a child again. He tells me he feels the presence of this child with him and he is embracing the childhood that was cut short for him. He is excited about how he feels and wants to learn how to journey for himself.

Dismemberment Journeys

Dismemberment journeys are an important ancestral ritual of a shaman's work. In many shamanic cultures, one may journey to offer oneself to be torn apart spiritually in order to be reborn. Dismemberment journeys allow us to break apart old thinking patterns, belief systems and a general sense of "stuckness". Asking compassionate guides for a dismemberment or receiving the gift of a spontaneous dismemberment journey brings renewal and rejuvenation and a better alignment of body, mind, and spirit.

Dismemberment Journey: Love

I am feeling out of sorts and out of balance. Please give me a teaching so that I can feel more balanced.

Celeste (2004)

Dismemberment Journey for Celeste: Love

I go to a place that is high above the clouds. It is so high I feel it is somewhere in the cosmos, no... somewhere beyond the cosmos. I enter a space where two rows of hooded figures stand facing each other. At the end of the rows, is seated another hooded figure. He asks me why I have come. I explain that I need his guidance, a teaching from him. He gets up and swiftly cuts my head off with a huge knife.

Again, he asks, *'Why are you here?'*

My head, now on the floor, responds, *'To ask for forgiveness. I am not worthy.'*

He stuffs a cloth in my mouth so that I cannot speak. Again, he asks, *'Why are you here?'*

Without saying a word, I share with him that I do not know. He then motions for me to sit down. I sit with the other cloaked figures. I see myself waking up and the whole

110

process repeats itself again and again—the questions, the beheading, the sitting. Then, as I sit there in silence, various people from different times in my life appear before me and stand in front of me. Each one of them says, *'I just want to be seen and loved.'*

The cloaked figure asks me if I have helped them in their journey. As he asks me this, my heart feels very small and hard like a stone. I mumble that I have not. I know that I have acted out of hate, jealousy, hurt, and pain. I ask each one of them for forgiveness.

The cloaked figures then dress me in a white robe. I climb up a mountain and enter a cave. There are two girls in the cave, one 12 and the other 5 years of age. I am surprised to see them there. They tell me that they have come to this cave because they did not like the feeling of being inside of me. They are scared. I ask them to come with me. I tell them it is safe now and that I cannot be whole if they are not with me. I tell them I am ready to love them and nurture them. They get up and take my hand and we walk down the mountain. They are protected by my cloak. The three of us return to the group of hooded figures. I stand before them and they start to blow air. As they blow, I feel the two little girls starting to merge with me. I kiss the little five-year-old and she enters my body through my mouth. I feel giddy. I hug the 12-year-old and she also enters my body through my stomach. They are now both a part of me. I am elated, and my heart is so expansive.

The cloaked figure says, *'You must take care of them now.'*

'How?' I ask.

'By being love, always,' he says.

Check-in with Celeste

After this journey I began an intensive journaling exercise. I began recollecting events in my childhood and noted down incidents and people that I had encountered. I noted down every person I felt I may have hurt consciously or unconsciously. This took months. When I thought I had finished, I began writing letters of forgiveness to the people on my list. Once I had finished these I proceeded to write letters of gratitude to the people on my list. I never sent any of the letters. I bundled up the letters and performed a private ceremony where I released all of the letters and incidents. As I watched it all burn, I felt a great sense of release and gratitude. I now take note of the hurt I may consciously or unconsciously cause to someone else and ask for forgiveness. I also begin every day by giving thanks for my life.

Dismemberment Journey: Renewal

I began my day with my usual practice of journeying to my guides and teachers. I was surprised and delighted to receive the gift of a dismemberment journey.

Celeste (2001)

Dismemberment Journey for Celeste: Renewal

I have been lying in the hot desert sun for three days and three nights. The bindings on my wrists and ankles are digging into my flesh. As the sun rises, my skin bakes and my body craves coolness. My lips are parched, and I can no longer speak. As the sun sets, my whole body shivers and craves heat. How low can one survive like this? Finally, on the fifth morning, when I think my ordeal cannot get any worse, a large black raven shows up. After taking stock of my helpless situation, Raven approaches me and perches itself on my red raw belly. Without haste and without warning, he plucks my eyes out and eats them. This, it seems, is the permission for other creatures to attack the rest of my body. At night, I can hear them scurry and slither. They start with my feet and hands, and when my skin is pierced and open, they feast on my belly and innards. When my body is almost decimated, I slip out and hover above it, watching the creatures gnawing away at my bones. It strikes me then, *'Who is doing the watching? Who am I if I am not this body?'* I am still here but I am not my body. I feel light and expansive and soar into the sky. I am not sure what to do. I fly around and around enjoying this new-found freedom. The old Mexican sees me flying around this way, so he lassoes me and shoves me into a cloth bag. He carries me like this, trapped in the bag, into a large luminous dome-like structure. He chants and hums, and starts concocting some kind of potion over a large fire. He gently takes me out of the bag and pours the potion on me. I have a body again, but it is very luminous and translucent. I am very fragile and weak. So, he leans me up underneath a willow tree to gather strength.

After seven days, I wake up fully energized. I join the Mexican who is still sitting by the fire. He has three bowls filled with various potions. He offers me the first bowl which contains a liquid so thin, it looks like wispy smoke. I gulp it down. I suddenly feel very light and bright. I become Nune Cara, healer of the spirit world. The old Mexican and a small mouse look at me and bow saying, *'We are honored to be in your presence.'*

The old Mexican then brings the second bowl. It is filled with a thick black liquid that looks like tar. I drink it, but it is bitter and it flows slowly down my throat. I suddenly feel very heavy and dragged down. The energy of the liquid is pulling me down. I ask the old Mexican why I need to drink this. He responds, *'Because it will ground you when you go to the other side: you need to be grounded.'*

He then offers me the third and last bowl. It is filled with a green liquid. It is tart and bitter to the tongue but also strangely refreshing and invigorating. I am suddenly full in my body. I feel balanced and whole. The old Mexican says, *'You are now ready to return, but before you do, here is a final gift.'* He hands me a tiny square of folded paper. He kisses my cheek and leaves. Now alone with the mouse, I unfold the paper carefully. Two simple words are written: *Love, Heal.*

I start to cry.

Check-in with Celeste

This journey is a beautiful example of the power of connecting with guides and spirits. By moving around my energy in a different way, my guides help me see the world with fresh eyes and a bigger heart. These journeys stay with me for a very long time and change me to the very core of my being in ways that words cannot describe

Dismemberment Journey: Initiation

Eagle Brother, please give me the gift of dismemberment.
Celeste (2008)

Dismemberment Journey for Celeste: Initiation

I visit Eagle Brother, my protector. We get on a black horse and ride for a very long time. We go to a place outside of time and space. We reach a large field where thousands of people are gathered. They welcome me. They wash my feet and cleanse me. I thank them and tell them I want to honor my gift and ask for their blessing. They remove all of my clothes. A group of women start writing symbols all over my body. Then, they tell me to walk into the fire. My entire body burns up.

I have a new body.

They write symbols all over my body again and they tell me to dive into the water. I do and feel myself drowning in the depths.

I have a new body.

They write symbols all over my body, and this time, they tell me to walk into the smoke. I do and feel myself rising up and up and up and dissipating into the air.

I have a new body.

They write symbols all over my body and, this time, they cover me with dirt and mud. The sun dries it all up and I slip out of the mud-like form.

I have a new body.

They etch a huge symbol on my heart. They say, *'Welcome.'* I dance and sing with them, and Eagle Brother.

Dismemberment Journey: Connection

What do I need in my life right now to feel more connected?

Celeste (2011)

Dismemberment Journey for Celeste: Connection

I start walking along the shore feeling numb and disconnected. A large dark horse gallops towards me and I climb on him. Then, a man riding a horse joins us and we ride in silence for a very long time. We ride beyond the beach, into a thick forest, through clearings, over hills, and through open fields. We finally reach a small village. The man guides me to the shaman's hut. He is brewing some kind of potion. He says that it takes three days to boil it down, then you have to sit for forty days and forty nights to see if the potion is good. He asks if I have that kind of patience. I say I do not. He turns to me and asks, *'What is your question?'*

I mumble, *'What do I need in my life right now to feel connected?'* As the words come out, it strikes me that my question shows my impatience, it now seems so unimportant. I continue, trying to explain how I feel, *'I feel*

118

so disconnected, off track; I want to know if I am on the right path.'

He sits there for a while then he gets up and says, 'You need to play.' We leave the hut and I notice the people of the village milling about. They look happy. I wonder how they know to be happy.

'Does their life have meaning?' I ask.

The shaman: 'You ask as if life itself is not meaning enough, you need to shed your shell to see better.' He then steps on my toe and I slip out of my body. I am a luminous being.

I start flowing. Eagle comes, and we fly together. We fly to the stars, we play in the sky. We fly to a field where little girls are playing. When they see me, they run to me and we hug and giggle. I am so alive and happy. But then I remember my question and I say, 'I feel like my light is fading.' They give me a mirror. I look like an old woman, crusty and wrinkled. They bring me to a river and they wash me and chip all of the crust away. They give me the mirror again and I now see a young girl with smooth skin. We return to the field and play until the sun sets.

Eagle brings me to a cave. There is an old man there, sleeping beside a fire. Eagle tells me that the old man can finally rest because I am there to stoke my fire. I am confused but do not say anything. Eagle says the old man has not slept peacefully in a while. Eagle leaves and the old man wakes up. I ask him why he stays in the cave to stoke my fire. He says, 'This is what I chose.'

I ask him, 'What happens if the fire goes out?'

He does not answer, then I say 'I die,' responding to my own question.

Check-in with Celeste

At times in my life, when I feel down and a tinge of self-pity, I am reminded by my guides of how everything I experience and perceive is a choice. I am not my pain, my sadness, my anger. If I want to feel something different, I can literally slip out of myself and experience something new. My guides remind me often of the power and importance of choosing joy and play, and how the illusion of separateness generates pain and suffering.

Dismemberment Journey: Heart of my Heart

Please give me permission to be a teacher for others.

Celeste (2003)

My guides bring me down a winding river in a long canoe. They are silent and it is dark. I sense we are going deeper and deeper into an Amazon-like jungle. We finally arrive at a place where there is a council of elders. They look like Incas or Mayans. I sit there and ask permission to be a teacher. The elder Inca approaches me and stares into my eyes for a long time. I stare back and do not flinch. He then reaches for my wrist and cuts it. He cuts his own wrist and brings our two slit wrists together. He says, *'Blood of my Blood.'*

I faint.

When I awake, I am surrounded by a council of elders in white robes. The lead elder approaches me and she opens my chest to reveal my heart. She then reaches in and writes symbols on my heart. Our energies connect and she says, *'Heart of my Heart.'*

I faint again.

When I awake, I become a ball of energy, in a circle with other balls of energy. We play around together spinning and dancing.

Suddenly, I am back in my body staring in the eyes of the Inca Elder. He says, *'Remember who you are; bring the children back to us.'*

Check-in with Celeste

As mentioned at the beginning of this book, for a long time I resisted doing this work. I felt I needed permission and affirmation from my spiritual guides and teachers. This journey was a resounding yes to the path I chose to embrace.

Dismemberment Journey:
Inner Child

Please connect me with my inner child.

Celeste (2001)

Dismemberment Journey for Celeste: Inner Child

I enter a cave where I find a child of about 7–8 years of age. I ask if she wants to come with me to meet someone. I gift her with a medicine pouch that I place around her neck. I take her little hand and we walk out of the cave into a field where I had first met my wild child. Mother Lion is there waiting for us. I tell Mother Lion that I want to connect with my inner child. Suddenly, I feel something foreign in my throat and start coughing until I spit it out. When it touches the ground, it looks like a black gooey blob but then it became a small black child. Lion tells us both to sit down back to back, the black child and me, with the little girl sitting on my lap. I follow her instructions but tell her I do not want to child to be harmed. I just want a healing but I do not want to hurt this little innocent child. I keep on talking until, exasperated, Mother Lion bites my head off and flings it aside. My head keeps on talking and talking, so

Lion goes to it and picks it up in her jaw and brings it far into the bush. Finally, everything is silent. Lion finishes binding us together and then I feel myself connecting with the gooey-like substance of the child. Suddenly, the black child jumps up and flips back and unties me. At the same time, I flip back and untie the child.

We start dancing and many ancestors join us and start dancing with us. They form a circle around us and one of them approaches the child and opens up her stomach. The elder scoops in and removes a lot of mud and dirt. As she scoops the child's stomach, I feel the mud oozing out of my own mouth, ears, eyes, and nose. I just keep on spewing out this blackness. When the child's stomach is cleansed, the elder fills it with clean water. As she does this, water is pouring out of my own mouth, ears, eyes, and nose. When the stomach is completely cleansed, the elder invites Lion to come and lick the stomach to make sure it is all clean. When Lion is finished, they lay the child in the sun and let the stomach dry. Then they fill it with air, light, and an array of beautiful colors. Then the child bounces up again. I ask Lion what was healed. The child simply says, *'I felt bad before, now I feel good. You have the right to be you.'*

I play with the black child and the little girl for a while under a huge willow tree. Then we climb into the branches of the willow tree, and she rocks us back and forth and sings to us.

Check in Journey with Celeste

This journey was both a dismemberment journey and a soul retrieval. In order to reconnect with my inner child and

my wild child, my current structure and configuration had
to be taken apart.

Death and Dying Journeys

Psycho-pomp work (*psycho-pomp is escorting souls to the after-life or helping deceased persons cross over*) is an important aspect of a shaman's work. Accompanying the dying in the dying process or helping family members letting go is a beautiful process. For most, death is a taboo subject, yet it is an integral part of our lives. Over the years I have done many journeys for clients who wish to "check-in" on a deceased or loved one, for clients who are dying and want to have someone help them cross over and for clients who feel they are still consciously or unconsciously "attached" to a deceased person.

Death and Dying Journey: Waiting

As part of my shamanic training, I journeyed to places like hospitals, mental health institutions and connect with energies to help them "cross over."

Celeste (2006)

I enter the hospital lobby. It is a swarm of noise and activity. Little islands of bustling energy and anxiety walking from one place to another. I notice a little old man sitting by himself on a bench. I sit beside him. He looks so sad and lost. After a while, I ask him if he is okay. He says he does not know what to do. He is waiting for his wife. She has told him to wait in the lobby until she comes back to get him. He tells me that he has been waiting for a very, very long time and he finally got so tired, he decided to just wait on the bench. I ask, if perhaps he could call her or ask someone from the hospital to help him. He says he has tried but that everyone is so busy, they just ignore him. I ask him how long he has been waiting. He says, *'I am not sure.'*

On a whim, I ask him, *'Do you know today's date?'*

In spite of the blustering snow outside, he responds, *'June 12th.'*

I look at him for a while then ask softly, *'What year is it?'*

He replies, *'1976.'*

I glimpse at the cell phone in my hand, and after another long pause I ask him, *'Do you know that you have died? Do you know that you are no longer bound by your body? You can leave it now, because it no longer serves you.'* He stares at me in shock. I see great fear and confusion in his tired gaze. I look into his eyes and ask, *'Do you want me to help you find your wife?'* He nods, tears streaming down his old cheeks. I take his hand and bring him to my guide who opens a door. A shaft of light beams through, engulfing both the old man and me. As we pass through it, the old man begins to shine. An old woman shows up, vibrating and shining.

The old man looks up and says, *'Why didn't you come to get me?'* She smiles, takes his hand and they both turn and leave merging into the light.

Death and Dying Journey: Waiting Ancestors

'Hello Celeste, I was wondering if you could do a journey for my father who is very ill.'

Susan (2018)

Journey for Susan's Father

I journey to Eagle Brother and ask him to bring me to René, Susan's father. He brings me to Grandmother Crocodile. We go to René, who is lying in a cave. Grandmother Crocodile approaches him and starts humming and making gestures with her hands around his body. She reaches into his stomach area and moves some energy around. She then blows energy in the stomach area. She goes to the throat area and massages it to open his voice so that he can speak more clearly. Then she moves on to his heart area and she opens up the heart cavity so that his heart could open itself up. She creates a passage between his heart and throat areas. She then goes to his head and she removes some webs and clinging things. She clears up his head area for quite a while. Then she moves to his feet and washes them and massages them. She then blows into his feet and then she blows into his crown. As she blows, she is opening up a clear channel for the energy to flow through René's body. As she does this, I can see energy flowing through the body. I then hear drumming and notice that, on the other side of the river, there are ancestors standing in a circle drumming, singing, and dancing. Grandmother then touches René's eyes and his heart and she says to him, *'It is time for you to see clearly with your heart. Use your time now to **be** your heart.'*

Check-in with Susan

A few days after this journey, Susan tells me that she drove to her father's house and read the journey to him. He asked her to read it several times and broke down every time. Susan informs me that her father is dying of cancer of the stomach and he was afraid of dying until this journey was read to him. She tells me he is very grateful and now at peace.

Several weeks after speaking with Susan, her father passed away peacefully.

Death and Dying Journey: My Mother, Jeanne

The following is a series of journeys I did leading up to and following my mother's death.

'Please give me permission to journey on behalf of my mother who has Alzheimer's. I want to see if there is anything I can do for her at this time.'

Celeste (June 2014)

1st Journey for Jeanne (June 6th, 2014   her birthday)

I journey to Eagle Brother and ask him if I can see my mother. I am expecting the usual answer denying me this request. For the past two years, I have asked permission to journey on behalf of my mother but my guides tell me I cannot. But this time, Eagle Brother nods. He takes my hand and we walk in a forest. We walk for quite a while. Suddenly he stops and turns to me. He puts his finger on his lips and motions for me to be very quiet. We emerge into a clearing. I see my mother in the clearing dancing all alone. I notice there is a cord attached around her waist. I follow the cord and see the other end is attached to my mother in her room in the retirement home. As she dances, she is very light and free. I am filled with emotion to see this beautiful woman so happy and unbound by the ugliness of her disease. I am about to leave and just as I am turning to go, I notice my deceased father on the other side of the clearing. He is watching my mother and smiling. When we return, I ask Eagle Brother if my mother is in pain and if there is anything I can do for her. He tells me this, *'Your mother is not in pain. She has unfinished business in this body. Her spirit is disconnecting from her and simply waiting until the body releases it. This will take the time it needs. You cannot do anything except care for the shell that was your mother.'* I thank him and return.

2nd Journey for Jeanne (Aug. 2015)

This journey was done on Monday morning at around 7:30–7:45. When I finished journeying and checked my messages, I learned that my mother had passed away that morning.

I journey to my usual sacred space to give thanks. When I get to the place where I usually honor the ancestors, I notice that no one is sitting on the ancestral blanket. For the past year, I have been seeing my deceased maternal grandmother and other deceased aunts and uncles. On the blanket now are empty plates and crumbs as if a picnic had taken place but was now finished. Grandfather Medicine comes to me and asks me to follow him. I take his hand, and he brings me to a clearing where I have seen my mother dancing. This time my mother is no longer dancing. She is kind of bent over. Grandfather tells me, *'She is finished with her dance.'* I ask if I can go near her. He says yes, but that I cannot touch her. I approach her and she sees me and says, *'J'ai fini de danser. J'ai fini là.'* (I am finished dancing; I am finished now.)

I respond, *'Tu peux t'en aller chez vous maintenant.'* (You can go home now.)

She looks up and says, *'Penses-tu que c'est correct? Est-ce que c'est correct?'* (Do you think that is okay? Is it okay for me to go now?)

I'm all choked up and I say, *'Oui maman, c'est correct tu peux partir là.'* (Yes, Mom. You can go home now.)

She hesitates for a bit and then she notices Grandfather Medicine. He offers her his hand, and she takes it. As she does this, I notice that the energetic cord that was attached to her body is starting to disintegrate. Grandfather and Mother start walking towards the forest. I then see my father come out of the forest. When my mother sees him, she smiles brightly. She then reaches my father and they embrace. As they embrace, I notice that my mother is starting to vibrate. Then a whole bunch of luminescent beings come out and surround my mother. She is vibrating brightly. I cannot really see her anymore but the whole group is humming and vibrating. It is breathtakingly beautiful.

3rd Journey for Jeanne
(Sept. 2015)

A few days after my mother has passed, I decide to do a check-in journey to see if she has completely crossed over.

Celeste

I journey to Grandfather Medicine. It is night time. He brings me to the field where I had last seen my mother. There is nothing there. It is very quiet. He tells me there is nothing here to see anymore. I ask him if I could see my mother. He says no. He explains that I cannot go where she has gone. He then points up to the stars and points out Ursa, the Bear Constellation. He says, *'Look for her there for a while. It's time to begin the release. You need to grieve like a daughter now.'*

I respond, *'It's hard to release right now.'*

He says, *'Release comes through grief. Feel the grief and then you will be able to release. Do not go to her for a while. You need to release now.'*

4th Journey for Jeanne (June 6th, 2018—her birthday)

I have tried unsuccessfully to journey to connect with Mother, until one morning on the day of her birthday I receive a gift.

Celeste

I walk in a desert for a long time and then arrive in the middle of nowhere where there is an old familiar hut. The

Old Mexican greets me and invites me to drink some clear liquid from a large bowl. He then tells me to go for a walk. I walk in the desert for a while and then I feel like I am in a different reality, like I am walking in some kind of gelatinous realm. Everything is very bright but the air is thick like Jello. I keep on walking and it feels nice. Everything around me gets brighter and brighter but still very gelatinous. I notice as I am walking, that the gelatin is removing some skin from my body, like a large exfoliating experience. I eventually emerge from this realm and a hand suddenly reaches out to me. I take the hand and look up to see my mother. She is about 30 years old and radiant. She smiles at me and we run together through a field. She brings me to this other realm where we are both pure energies, like grains of sand. We swirl together and make this kind of sandstorm, my sand mixing with hers. I feel her inside me. We then return to our forms and she stands before me. She removes my heart and gives me a new one. She then removes my hands and gives me new ones. I could sense my father's presence on the edges but I sense that this is a gift from my mother. She looks at me and says, *'It is now time to use your hands, let your heart speak through your hands, not your head. Use the gift I have given you.'* Then she disappears.

I am suddenly back in the hut with the Old Mexican, holding the bowl of water he has given me.

Death and Dying Journey: My Father, Edouard

The following is a series of journeys I did leading up to and following my father's death.

In May 2009, my father asked me to journey for him. My father was intrigued by shamanism and had tried to journey on several occasions but was never successful. He would occasionally ask me to "go check in on him."

Celeste (2009)

1ˢᵗ Journey for Edouard (May 2009)

I journey to Grandfather and ask him about Edouard. Grandfather is silent for a bit then he takes my hands in his. He stares into my eyes and says, *'You need to start the process of detaching. Your father's time has come. You will not enjoy his company for very long now. Help him get ready.'*

I was stunned. After the journey, I immediately called my father and told him I wanted to come and visit. As we sat on his back deck, I shared the brief journey I had done for him. He remained quiet for a long time, then he said, 'I think I may be dying. Do not tell your mother. I am not feeling good and I sense that I am close to my time.' That afternoon, I agreed to help him prepare for his death. In June of the same year, my father was diagnosed with stage-4 cancer.

2nd Journey for Edouard (Aug. 2009)

I journey to Grandfather Medicine and ask him if he has any guidance for my father as he prepares for his crossing over. Grandfather Medicine gives me this message for my father: *'It is time now to let go of everything. You must literally lose your mind and start resting into your heart. The mind no longer needs to know and does not need to control. Open your heart, as it truly is and show your heart to others.'*

I did several journeys like these for my father. This one was particularly powerful for him. As I shared it with him, he told me that when he had awakened that morning there was a small heart-shaped stone by his bedside. He asked my mother who had placed the stone there. My mother said no one had come since the night before and she had cleaned the room that morning and there was no stone there. My father was deeply touched by this and told me he felt it was Grandfather Medicine telling him he was with him.

3rd Journey (December 1st, 2009)

My father and I spoke often about the day of his death and he made me promise that I would be there at his side

137

and that I would help him cross over. I did many journeys
for him that summer and fall. The following journey is the
crossing over journey I did with my father.

I am both, in the room where my father is dying
surrounded by my siblings and my mother, and in a field. I
am drumming gently so that my father's essence can follow
the beat. Suddenly, I see a group of white-robed people
coming out of the forest and entering the clearing. This is
my signal to change the drumbeat. As my drum carries me
into the clearing, I am no longer in the room but in this
clearing. And then, I see my father's form walking into the
clearing. He has the shape of my father but he is translucent
and luminescent. The people see him and greet him,
laughing, and hugging him. He is very happy to be there.
They create a circle around him and he starts to dance. He
seems to be so happy. He has no pain and he is dancing
around like a young boy. Then, the circle opens and
Grandfather Medicine shows up. My father immediately
recognizes him and walks to him. Grandfather nods and
says, *'Welcome home, Son.'*

My father takes Grandfather's hand and then hugs him.
He is so happy to finally see him again. Grandfather
motions for my father to follow him. My father starts to
walk with him but then, he stops as if he has forgotten
something. He turns around and he stares at me. He
hesitates. He begins to start walking towards me. I sob and
choke, unable to contain my emotion. Then I drum harder
and say to him, *'Vas-y papa, vas-y! C'est correct, vas-y!'*
(Go, Dad, go! It's okay, go!) He then smiles, looks at

Grandfather and enters the forest with him. The circle of greeters leaves and enters the forest. I am now all alone.

After I finish my journey and stop my drumming, I come back into the room and notice my siblings crying. My sister, who is a nurse, tells me our father has passed. She adds that my drumbeat changed at exactly the moment that he let out his last breath. I go to another room and sit in silence for a long time. I am both very sad and elated.

4th Journey (Sept. 2010)

Before he died, my father told me that he would try to connect with me "from the other side." For days and months after his passing, I tried to journey to him but my guides told me it was too soon. They said, 'You need to grieve as a daughter now.' I was very angry at my father because I felt he had broken his pact. I eventually let go of this anger, understanding that this was part of the grieving process. Then one day, almost a year after my father's death, I had the most amazing journey.

Celeste

I journey to Grandfather Medicine and ask for a teaching. He does not respond and motions for me to follow him. We walk into a forest and reach Crone's house. She hugs me and gives me a liquid to drink so that I can remain invisible. She then puts a cloak on me. I leave again with Grandfather and we get to a river. We get into a canoe and Grandfather paddles down the river. He is insistent that I remain very quiet. He explains that he is bringing me to a place where very few people go and that this is a gift to me from my father. I am surprised because I had not felt my father's energy since his passing and had been told not to journey to him. We continue down the river until we get to a desert. We leave the canoe and start walking in the desert. We cross various rivers and landmarks in silence. Then we reach a place where thousands of energetic beings are gathered around a large protruding stone. They are all looking up at the stone in silence. I am about to ask what is going on and Grandfather places a finger on my lips. I nod in understanding. Grandfather and I are now standing on top of the protruding rock, overlooking the expansive desert and the beings below. I see several luminescent beings dancing around. It is very beautiful to watch. To my surprise, I notice that one of the beings is my father. He is dancing this intricate dance. I am so excited to see him. As he is dancing, he is swirling, like a ball of energy. He begins to spin faster and faster, swirling upward into a spiral until he spins so fast that he goes straight up and disappears. I am deeply moved, but I am uncertain as to what I have just witnessed. When all of the beings have finished dancing and have spiraled upward, Grandfather and I leave the desert and return to the canoe. When we have returned to the forest, Grandfather finally speaks, *'You have witnessed your father's transitioning. He has given you the gift of his transcendence. Very few are allowed to witness this process and return to their human lives.'* I have many questions, but instead of asking them I offer my gratitude and say how deeply honored I am to have been given this gift. I thank Grandfather. But, just as I am ready to leave, I hear a wolf howl in the distance. I smile and then laugh out loud; I know that this is my father.

After this journey, my father started coming to me as a Wolf. He would show up in my journeys to provide guidance and teachings. He told me he was no longer Edouard and could not show up this way for me. Wolf has become a great teacher for me.

Death and Dying Journey:
Releasing

After my father crossed over, I felt a deep ache and sense of loss. I went through all of the stages of grief, but still found it hard to let him go. Several years after his passing, I felt it was time to ask my guides to help me release him.

Celeste

I go to the Tree of Life to meet the three Wyrd Sisters. I sit against the massive trunk and wait. After a while, they appear and offer me three fruits: a date, an apple, and a seed. I eat all three. I ask the Sisters if they can help me release the pain of my father's death. They bring me to a cave. They take water from a pool and tell me to drink one single drop. One of them then removes a small strand from my tapestry. Part of the tapestry still has the strand but the edge of the tapestry does not. She then wraps the strand she has removed around my heart and tells me, that this is where I need to keep my father. I thank her. We return to the Tree and we surround it. Each one of us is facing a direction: north, south, east, and west. We then connect with light and energy and the Tree of Life lights up. They then bring me to a pool of water by the tree and tell me to strip down and wash myself in the pool. They give me strict instructions not to drink the water. I swim in the pool, and when I emerge, I am glowing. They tell me that I am now imbued with their healing power and that we are now bound. One of the sisters takes a length of thread and wraps it around my finger. As she does this, I become huge and expansive. They then tie the thread around their own fingers. We circle the Tree and again we light up and again the Tree lights up. I thank them and return, my heart much lighter than before.

Conclusion
The Dance Begins

There is a starting place

Where you read many, many books

Where you listen to many, many teachers

Where you take copious notes

Where you follow the recipe given

Then, something happens,

And you burn all of your notes, and you close all of the books, and you thank all of the teachers, and you begin to rely on Spirit.

And then… the dance begins.

Celeste

www.ingramcontent.com/pod-product-compliance
Lightning Source LLC
Chambersburg PA
CBHW060938040426
42445CB00011B/914